J.L. GRANATSTEIN is one of Canada's best-known historians. Among his many books are *The Ottawa Men: The Civil Service Mandarins, 1935–1957*; *Canada 1957–1967: The Years of Uncertainty*; and, with David Bercuson and William Young, *Sacred Trust? Brian Mulroney and the Conservative Party in Power*.

In these lively, timely, and contentious essays J.L. Granatstein takes on one of the 'hoary central myths' of Canadian history and historiography: that the Liberals sold out Canada to the United States. It is a myth, he claims, perpetuated by Conservative historians such as Donald Creighton and George Grant, and by socialists like James Laxer. The original villain of this long-running melodrama is not the Liberals, the author maintains, but Britain.

Focusing on events surrounding the first and second world wars and the Cold War, Granatstein argues that Canadian governments, both Liberal and Conservative, turned to the south for economic ties only when their efforts to form such ties with Britain failed, and for defence only when Britain was too weak to guarantee Canadian security.

As Canadians continue to argue with each other about the benefits of a cosier relationship with our American cousins, Granatstein provides a salutary reminder that the historical roots of the debate stretch not only across the forty-ninth parallel but back across the Atlantic too.

How Britain's Weakness Forced Canada into the Arms of the United States

The 1988 Joanne Goodman Lectures

J.L. GRANATSTEIN

University of Toronto Press
Toronto Buffalo London

Canadian Cataloguing in Publication Data

Granatstein, J.L., 1939–
How Britain's weakness forced Canada into the
arms of the United States

(The 1988 Joanne Goodman lectures)
Includes index.
ISBN 0-8020-5837-x (bound) ISBN 0-8020-6746-8 (pbk.)

1. Canada – Relations – Great Britain. 2. Great
Britain – Relations – Canada. 3. Canada – Relations
– United States. 4. United States – Relations –
Canada. I. Title. II. Series: The Joanne
Goodman lectures; 1988.

FC245.G73 1989   327.71041   C89-093592-0
F1029.5.G7G73 1989

The Joanne Goodman Lecture Series

has been established by Joanne's family

and friends to perpetuate the memory of her

blithe spirit, her quest for knowledge, and

the rewarding years she spent at the

University of Western Ontario.

For Richard Preston and Theodore Ropp

Contents

Foreword

The Joanne Goodman Lectures were established at the University of Western Ontario in 1975 to honour the memory of the elder daughter of Mr and Mrs Edwin A. Goodman of Toronto. Each year the university invites a scholar to deliver three lectures on some aspect of the history of the English-speaking people, particularly those of the Atlantic Triangle of Canada, the United Kingdom, and the United States, that will be of interest to members of the university community and the general public. The list of those who have so far participated in the series indicates the distinction of these lectures and the part they play in the intellectual life of the institution. The University of Western Ontario is grateful to Mr and Mrs Goodman and their family and friends for this generous and moving benefaction dedicated to a student who loved history and enjoyed her years at this university.

Professor J.L. Granatstein of York University is one of Canada's best known and most prolific historians. In the past twenty years he has written or edited over two dozen books and established an unrivalled mastery of the political and diplomatic archives. He has also the great ability to relate history to present concerns. All of these qualities were reflected in the topical lectures which we at the University of Western Ontario were fortunate to hear in the midst of the excitement of a general election on free trade. Nor do the lectures lose their contemporary relevance after the election, for, as Professor Granatstein amply demonstrates here, events have a way of turning out ironically with results quite different from those imagined by people who made the decisions.

Neville Thompson
The University of Western Ontario

Preface

Joanne Goodman, a second-year history student at the University of Western Ontario, died in an automobile crash on Highway 401 in April 1975. The immediate shock of loss thankfully dulls the initial suffering, but there can be no pain more severe or more prolonged for parents than that brought on by the death of a dearly loved child. Only memory survives to temper that pain, and memories, however happy, are wholly inadequate to ease the contemplation of what might have been, of what should have been.

I commend Mr and Mrs Goodman and their relatives and friends for deciding to commemorate their daughter with a lecture series. Since their inception in 1976, the Joanne Goodman Lectures have become the most important series of annual historical lectures offered in Canada. It is a great honour for me to have been asked to give them and to join such mentors, colleagues, friends, and distinguished scholars as Charles Stacey, Carl Berger, and Desmond Morton as Joanne Goodman lecturers.

JLG

The imagery of Canada as a woman sought by Cousin Jonathan (or Uncle Sam) goes back to the immediate post-Confederation period.

A Pertinent Question

Mrs Britannia: 'Is it possible, my dear, that you have ever given your cousin Jonathan any encouragement?'

Miss Canada: 'Encouragement! Certainly not, Mamma. I have told him we can *never* be united.'

Coming Home from the Fair

Brother Jonathan: 'Adieu, fair Canada. I have long adored you, but never so much as now. May I not hope some day to claim you as my own?'

Canada (*kindly but firmly*): 'Never. I hope always to respect you as my friend and well-wisher, but can never accept you as my lord and master. Farewell.'

The Reciprocity election of 1911 raised Canadian fears about American designs on this country. This cartoon from the Toronto *Daily News* illustrates the theme.

Uncle Sam: 'I can almost hear them singing "The Star Spangled Banner" in Ottawa, Be gosh.'

Sir Robert Borden had successfully resisted reciprocity in 1911, but the Great War forced him to the United States for economic aid.

Canada always seemed to be someone's choreboy in cartoons – either Laurier's Canada helping Uncle Sam by rowing the reciprocity boat in 1911 or Borden's Canada aiding Britain with naval defence in 1912.

1911: Helping Uncle

1912: Helping Father

Prime Minister Bennett, seen here addressing the Imperial Economic Conference in Ottawa in 1932, tried hard to improve empire trade. Success was limited, however, and at the end of his term Bennett was scrambling to strike a trade deal with Washington.

As France fell and Britain came into dire peril in 1940, cartoonist Ivan Glassco expressed the fervent hope of Canadians.

Nervous One: 'Will she weather this, captain?' Skipper Churchill: 'Weather what?'

The Ogdensburg Agreement of 1940 was viewed darkly by Winston Churchill, who resented Canada's scuttling to save itself. He and Mackenzie King, seen here at Quebec in 1943, worked together during the war but were never soul-mates.

The Second World War took Canada out of Britain's defence sphere and put it into the United States'. By the Quebec Conference of 1943, when King posed with Roosevelt, Churchill, and the governor general, the Earl of Athlone, the transition was already history.

Louis St Laurent, shown here when he became Liberal leader in 1948, presided over the great inflow of American investment into Canada.

C.D. Howe, the 'Minister of Everything,' shown here opening a Bethlehem Steel Corporation operation in Picton, Ontario, in 1955. Howe believed if the choice was American investment and trade or no trade and investment, he was strongly for the former.

John Diefenbaker, here in a characteristic pose, tried to block British entry to the Common Market. With Charles de Gaulle's help, he succeeded – just at the time his government fell.

1

Paved
with Good
Intentions

MY TITLE for these essays is deliberately melodramatic. When I thought of framing them in this fashion, I readily admit that the vision I had was of a Victorian landlord, twirling his mustaches and twisting his lips into a sneer as he drove a poor but virtuous young woman out of her threadbare lodgings and towards a life of ill-repute. 'The rent, I must have the rent,' the landlord would say. 'I can't pay the rent,' our heroine would reply. 'You must pay the rent or ...' 'Or ...' being too awful for the woman to contemplate, it was out into the cold. Virtue triumphed for a time, but eventually poverty forced her into difficult circumstances, always the potential prey of another who had long coveted her.

Melodramatic, yes, but contentious and serious too. My purpose is to examine one of the hoary central myths of Canadian history and historiography: that the Liberals sold out Canada to the United States. This, I will argue by focusing on the Great War, the Second World War, and the early Cold War years, is largely incorrect. Canadian governments, both Conservative *and* Liberal, turned to the south only when their efforts to form a viable economic link with Great Britain failed. They turned to the Americans for defence only when Britain was too weak to guarantee Canadian security. It was less a Canadian desire to share Washington's bed, in other words, than London's impotence that compelled our seeking shelter within Uncle Sam's all-encompassing embrace.

No explanation of events is or can be monocausal, of course. There were many factors at work in the interplay of forces in the North Atlantic Triangle, and I do not claim for one moment that this explanation is the solitary correct one. There were Canadians who struggled long and hard to extricate Canada from the empire for fear of the impact of British wars on Canadian unity. There were Americans in and out of government who had economic and political designs on Canada. There was the inexorable pull of continental economics and geography, as well as the gentler but no less strong familial influences of intermarriage across an open border. What I will claim, however, is that the British aspect of the Canadian-American question has been neglected in the explanations thus far offered.

Nor do I accuse the British of willingly destroying the possibility of a separate Canadian nationhood in this century. The British, I must make clear at once, were not deliberately trying to force Canada into American hands during the two world wars and the Cold War that I will examine. For much of the period I am treating in these essays, that development was directly at variance with London's long-term interests. Britain's immediate and only intent during the world wars and after was to do everything it could to keep itself out of enemy control and its economy functioning. A great power that properly put its own interests first, and one of utter ruthlessness *in extremis*, Great Britain did only what it had to do.[1] The effects of British actions on Canada's course, nonetheless, were pronounced.

To say that this interpretation is at cross-purposes with one of the main currents of Canadian historiography is to understate matters. Consider the late W.L. Morton's *Kingdom of Canada*, which bemoaned British Canada's succumbing to the forces of pernicious Americanization.[2] On another occasion Morton was as harsh as any Canadian historian has ever been: Mackenzie King's 'persistent extension of Canadian autonomy without any positive counter-undertaking was in effect to destroy that European counterpoise, once military and next moral, by which Canada had balanced, or offset, the influence of the United States. King thus prepared the present condition of Canada, in which the country is so irradiated by the American presence that it sickens and threatens to dissolve in a cancerous slime.'[3] Cancerous slime indeed! How Europe's *moral* counterpoise was to protect us from Americanization Morton did not suggest.

Another notable and influential work was the late George Grant's *Lament for a Nation*, a brilliant, biting assault on Liberal continentalism and on those who 'never grant that the seeds of

Canada's surrender lay in Mackenzie King's regime.' To Grant, 'The British connection had been a source of Canadian nationalism. The west-east pull of trade ... provided a counter-thrust to the pull of continentalism. It depended on the existence of a true North Atlantic triangle.' Grant, unlike Morton, at least recognized that London could be at fault on occasion. It was John Diefenbaker's fate, he noted, 'to be in charge of the Canadian government at the time that the English ruling class had come to think of its Commonwealth relations as a tiresome burden.'[4] In that at least, as we shall see, he was correct.

But the main scholar responsible for popularizing the Liberal demonology was, of course, Donald Grant Creighton, the major Canadian historian of this century. In his writings on Sir John A. Macdonald, Creighton had understood, as did the Old Chieftain, that 'A rough balance of power within the English-speaking world seemed essential ... to ensure Canada's survival. The diplomatic and military support of Great Britain could alone offset the political preponderance of the United States.' As Creighton wrote, Macdonald proposed 'therefore to bring in the old world to redress the balance in the new.'[5] But Creighton came to realize, as did so many others, that Britain could not redress the imbalance in power in the new world. What then? Here is Creighton's interpretation of Canadian history since Confederation, put forward calmly and in a relatively non-polemical fashion in 1970 in *Canada's First Century*:

The purposes of the Fathers [of Confederation] were political and social as well as economic. Their primary object had been the establishment of a separate British-American nation and an independent northern economy based on a transcontinental east-west axis. From the first they had been acutely aware of the fact that the preponderating power of the United States and its instinct for continental domination represented the greatest danger to their main ambition; and they had realized equally clearly that the political connection with Great Britain gave them an ally whose support could alone redress the ominous imbalance of power on the North American continent.

For half a century, Britain provided markets, capital, immigrants, and diplomatic protection. For half a century, Canadians held to the belief that membership in the British Empire, which had ensured their own survival as a nation, would in the end enable them to play an influential part in world affairs. This first phase of the national existence lasted down until the First World War; but thereafter its essential elements began to decay or were deliberately impaired. The main direction of Canadian economic activity shifted from east to south. The American market became increasingly important in Canadian trade and American capital increasingly dominant in Canadian development. Along with this gradual dwindling of the old economic ties with the United Kingdom there went a corresponding decline in the historic Anglo-Canadian alliance and the virtual dissolution of the British Commonwealth. Mackenzie King, the archetypal Canadian continentalist, broke up the Britannic union without even attempting to devise policies for a separate and independent Canada. Since 1940, Canada has stood alone, its independence exposed to the penetrative power of American economic and military imperialism, its identity subjected to the continual hammering of American mass media.[6]

Every Canadian historian would agree with some of this reasoning, but for the most part it is simple nonsense. British action or inaction nowhere plays a part in events as described by Creighton, and Canada is assumed throughout to have had freedom of action, the ability to make meaningful choices. That, however, was precisely what the Canadian governments of this century did not often have.

Conservative historians blame the Liberal party, and especially Mackenzie King, for destroying British influence in North America, for allowing the Commonwealth link to be still-born, and for accelerating and welcoming Canada's slow, steady drift into the grip of the colossus to the south. Because of their long pre-eminent position in the field, their many textbooks, and the continuing influence of their former students, this conservative interpretation has become widely accepted. It has found favour on the left as well through its anti-American and anti-Liberal overtones, and writers such as Kari Levitt, James Laxer, and Melville Watkins have adopted much the same line.[7] It is, I think, fair to say that this Creightonian view of Canadian history has become and remains a truism. The 'plot folk,' as one colleague calls them, have had their conspiracy thesis accepted as truth.

It scarcely matters that Creighton, Morton, Grant, and Laxer could not by any stretch of the imagination be called specialists in the history of Anglo-American-Canadian relations in the twentieth century. Nor does it carry much weight that the few genuine specialists in this field do not accept their conclusions. What does matter is that Creighton et al. have had their partisan interpretation adopted and accepted, so much so that it is a staple of student essays. Journalists also delight in parroting the line. The egregious Charles Lynch, for example, noted the centenary of Mackenzie King's birth in 1974 with a column that denounced him as 'a compromiser, an appeaser, a sort of fat Neville Chamberlain, with guile,' and the Canadian leader responsible for 'transferring us from the bosom of the British mother onto the bony lap of the American uncle.'[8] That, at least, was a splendid phrase.

Like many truisms Canadians cherish, this Mortonian-Creightonian-Lynchian stance is not true; or, at least, not wholly true. That Canada has come increasingly under the Americans' political, economic, and military sway I must accept. That Liberal governments were in power during much of the period in which this process occurred is certainly correct. But that Mackenzie King, Louis St Laurent, and Lester Pearson collaborated in or willed this surrender to United States control is ridiculous. We must look at why events took place to understand what happened, and that is the purpose of these essays.

There is a definite resonance for our own time in the great reciprocity debate of 1911. The story is a familiar one for us all. When Finance Minister W.S. Fielding and Sir Wilfrid Laurier presented the agreement secretly negotiated with the United States to the House of Commons, Robert Borden and his Conservatives opposition sat stunned on their benches. The Liberals had done what every government since Confederation had tried and failed to do. But when the Ontario and Quebec Tory MPs returned to their constituencies they were astonished to discover that manufacturers and businessmen were frightened and unhappy, seeing reciprocal trade in natural products, almost all that was covered in the agreement, as the thin edge of the wedge. Free trade in manufactured goods was sure to follow, and that was certain to be bad for their hitherto protected businesses. In a few months, a powerful anti-free trade lobby was in the field, key Liberals in Toronto and elsewhere in Ontario had stopped following Laurier's white plume, and, by the time of the federal election later that year, the Quebec prime minister was damned throughout the Maritimes, Westmount, Ontario, and the West as a French-Canadian Catholic selling out British Canada to the hated Yankees. How times changed within the Conservative and Liberal parties by 1988!

My reason for beginning with 1911 is simply to remind readers that Borden and his party were defenders of the old National Policy, opponents of reciprocity, and, as strong, sometimes fervent supporters of the empire, cool to the United States.[9] For them, Canada was British, a state of mind that became ever more clear after Borden tried to get aid to the Royal Navy through the Commons (only to be blocked by a Liberal Senate, yet another echo that comes down through the years) and after he led Canada into the Great War in August 1914. Canada was British, and Canada was (to quote Laurier in 1914, not Borden) 'ready, aye ready' to assist Britain in this war for civilization, democracy, and, of course, empire.

But the Great War changed the constellation of power in the world. The cost of a twentieth-century total war was staggering in human life and in national wealth. In two years, Britain went from being an extraordinarily wealthy great power to a nation in serious financial difficulty. In the same period, the United States, though still neutral, saw its bankers and its bond and stock merchants swallow up investment territory that had hitherto been British. The British trade deficit with the United States burgeoned, and London had to sell off a vast portion of its investments in America to cover the shortfall and to get its hands on u.s. dollars. Moreover, Britain (as well as France and other Allies) had to borrow large sums on the New York market, again to get the dollars to pay for greatly expanded wartime trade with the United States. Wall Street, in other words, rose towards equality with The City.

That shift in economic power had a major impact on Canada. In the summer of 1914, London had had no foreboding of such events. So rich was Britain at the onset of the war that it could agree to finance Canada's war costs for food and war supplies in Britain and France. That seemed necessary because Canada was not a wealthy country, and the dominion government had only a strictly limited capacity to raise money. The federal budget in the last full year of peace, in fact, was $184 million, with most of the government's revenue coming, naturally enough, from the tariff. As important, Thomas White, the minister of finance, did not believe that government bonds could be marketed in Canada. In the circumstances, it seemed right and proper for London to carry Canada's war effort. 'We were leaning upon the British Treasury, not only for our war expenditure in England,' White wrote after the war, 'but also in Canada, and for part of our public works and railway expenditure as well ... The pound sterling was still king.'[10] Surely this conflict could not last long, and London and Ottawa and the thousands flocking to the colours all agreed that the war would be over by Christmas 1914.

But Christmas came and went, and so too did London's ability to raise enough money to pick up Canada's tab, along with all the other costs of the war. Indeed, by late November, White was beginning to realize that Canada had to assume a greater share of the war's costs. He had been offered a loan in New York, he told London, 'but on sentimental grounds and on account [of the] pride London has had in furnishing [the] Dominion [with] money [I] think [the] American market should be left to our Provinces and municipalities.'[11]

Sentiment and pride were wonderful things, but alone they could not pay the bills. By the summer of 1915, as the Bank of England struggled to keep up the value of the pound, Britain's exchange difficulties were such that the Treasury began urging Ottawa to raise a loan in Canada backed by imperial guarantees, an unheard-of suggestion. In November, nonetheless, Ottawa did float a war loan in Canada, and White was greatly surprised at the ease with which money poured in. The amount raised simply astonished him.

Moreover, and more significantly for our story, White cabled London on 2 July to ask the Treasury's views of a Canadian government loan from American sources. 'On account of the cessation of borrowing abroad,' he noted, 'a heavy strain has been thrown on the Canadian banks in financing provinces, municipalities, railways and other corporations whose securities normally would be sold in London.' Sir George Perley, the acting high commissioner in London, noted that he 'Personally favour[ed an] American loan if [it is] possible [to] take care [of] your requirements instead [of] borrowing here just now.' And on 22 July White told London that he had placed 'forty million dollars [in] one and two year notes' in New York at 5 and 5¼ per cent, respectively, though the 'negotiation [was] exceedingly difficult.'[12] The loan, he added later, 'was regarded with much satisfaction in Great Britain and Canada.'[13] There would be many further loans before the war ended and the United States displaced Great Britain as the Canadian lender of first resort.[14]

July 1915, therefore, was a critical month in Canada's history, though it has been little noted. For the first time the dominion government had turned to New York to meet its financial needs. For the first time the slightly raffish and less experienced American financiers had been called upon to lend Ottawa the money that the City of London could not.[15] Canada had come to a significant parting of the financial ways, and significantly the move had been made by the Conservative government of Sir Robert Borden whose devotion to empire was not in doubt. By 1916, 65 per cent of Canadian bond issues found buyers in the United States.[16]

Why was this necessary? The reason is clear. British financial markets had become so pressed by the demands of the first year of war that they could no longer meet all Canada's expenses overseas or be the source of funds to support the mounting costs of Canada's domestic and war expenditures. As White explained, 'Our object was to meet [the] wishes of [the] Treasury and relieve [the] London market and assist [the] exchange situation.'[17] It was Britain's economic difficulties, in other words, that turned Canada towards New York.

There was a similar shift in focus in the area of munitions and war supplies. After false starts in war production under the minister of militia and defence, Sir Sam Hughes, and his corrupt cronies on the Shell Committee, Sir Joseph Flavelle and the Imperial Munitions Board took hold and made Canada's munitions factories hum. The IMB was an imperial agency operating in Canada, in effect a purchasing agent for the British government. The IMB placed orders for the goods London needed and London paid for them – so long as it was able to do so. As early as mid-1915 the British had told Ottawa that they could no longer pay the total cost for Canadian war supplies, and Canadian aid had to be proffered. Sir Thomas White's solution was to use the over-subscription of the war loan of November 1915 as an advance to help Britain cover the costs of its purchases in Canada.[18]

The British tried repeatedly to get the Canadian government

to pay a continuing and substantial proportion of the IMB's operating costs, but White was always reluctant.[19] 'It would be a serious mistake to make any definite engagement,' the cautious former banker told Flavelle in late 1916. 'We can only take up the situation from time to time in Canada and arrange such credits as may be possible having regard to the condition of the banks and our finances.'[20] That was not and could not be good enough for the increasingly desperate British who, along with their allies, were now regularly forced to go on bended knee to Washington for assistance with their shortage of dollars. By April 1917, as America finally came into the war to end war as an 'associated power,' inter-Allied war credits amounted to $4.3 billion, of which 88 per cent had been covered by the British. Thereafter, the American government provided dollar credits to London, with the result that Great Britain became completely dependent on the United States.[21] A member of the financial mission seeking loans in the United States cabled to London that 'Members of the Cabinet should understand that our attitude towards the United States Government is that of beggars.'[22]

Britain's plight and the United States' economic strength inevitably had serious implications for Canada. In the late spring of 1917, while the Canadian public was still hailing the Canadian Corps' capture of Vimy Ridge and staring in shock at the casualty lists that epic event engendered, the British government told Ottawa that it could no longer afford to pay for goods from Canada. In effect, London said, if Canada wanted to keep up its sales of munitions, grain, hay, bacon, and cheese in the British market, it had to pay the costs.

This was the most serious advice the Conservative Borden government could have received. An end to agricultural sales meant irate farmers and meat-packers; an end to munition sales translated into urban unemployment; both implied serious political problems in a year that was almost certain to see a general election. And London knew what it was doing. The colonial secretary had telegraphed Ottawa on 30 June that 'Some risks must be taken. It is for the Canadian Government to weigh disadvantages of the course of action which we now urge upon them with the effect on the British Army's supply of munitions and the loss and confusion in which Canadian manufacturers would be involved if the IMB were not in a position to meet their liabilities.'[23] Prime Minister David Lloyd George added his weight to the British case in a message to Borden: the only alternatives are 'that we should largely diminish orders placed in Canada or that Canada should make itself mainly responsible for financing those orders. We should be most reluctant to adopt the former course.'[24]

The British were essentially blackmailing Canada into picking up the costs of a portion of the supplies Canada was sending to Britain. And the government, knowing that the Canadian public, for sentimental and material reasons, simply would not understand a refusal to do so, agreed to put up $25 million a month for the next six months to pay for a portion of the war exports.[25] But Ottawa was adamant that London provide $15 million U.S. dollars each month to Canada.[26] White's reasoning was clear: the war had greatly increased Canadian imports from the United States, notably in machine tools and components to be incorporated into munitions being exported to Britain. In years of rampant inflation, Canada's trade deficit with the United States had mounted enormously – estimates that it would reach $377 million in 1917 were circulating through Ottawa – and American dollars were in short supply, or so White believed.[27] The more Canada tried to do to help Britain, the deeper into the hole it went with the United States. Moreover, White wanted one more thing: a guarantee that Canada would be exempted from the ban on private foreign borrowing imposed by the United States when it came into the war.

White and the British were successful in meeting Canada's demands. The finance minister persuaded U.S. treasury secretary W.G. McAdoo to allow Canada to place a private loan in the United States. If Canada had American dollars, White told the American, Canadian purchases in the United States could continue; moreover, the United States had such great resources that it could afford to allow its smaller neighbour and good friend to be exempted from the general prohibition on loans.[28] McAdoo agreed in July 1917. White had struck the right note in a letter to McAdoo: 'We have in your time and mine always been good neighbors. Occasionally a verbal brickbat has been thrown across the fence but we have always sympathized with each other when brickbats have come from any foreign source. In our attitude towards constitutional liberty and all social problems our people are very much alike and understand each other better I think than any other two peoples in the world today. The struggle in a common cause will I am sure greatly cement our friendship and respect for each other.'[29]

Canadians and Americans, this leader of the anti-reciprocity campaign of 1911 now maintained, were almost the same. Significantly, however, White wanted a private loan, not one from the United States government. 'We shall have to pay a fairly stiff rate of interest,' he explained to a colleague, 'but I believe I would rather do this than borrow directly from the Government of the United States even at a lower rate of interest. In other words,' he maintained, 'I would rather we should "hoe our own road."'[30] With his insistence on borrowing on the private market, White had managed to preserve a limited freedom of action for the Canadian government. What was striking, nonetheless, was the extent of Canadian dependence on the United States. A few months later, British negotiators won a concession from Washington that saw Canada get the $15 million u.s. dollars each month, from American loans to Britain, to pay for the raw materials and components necessary for the production and export of Canadian war material overseas.

Moreover, as munitions production in Canada began to tail off despite the American assistance, Sir Joseph Flavelle of the Imperial Munitions Board (now popularly and contemptuously known as 'His Lardship,' thanks to profiteering charges levelled at his own meat-packing companies) turned to the Ordnance Department of the War Department in Washington for orders that could keep up employment in Canada and prevent the re-export of tools and dies back to the United States. By November 1917 a deal had been struck, and u.s. orders for munitions would now come to Canada.[31] This, the *Financial Post* noted, was 'the most important development of the past three months,' one that seemed certain to keep up war orders and war employment in the crucial months before the federal election in December.[32] Ultimately, the American orders proved disappointingly small, but the psychological – and political – boost provided by the IMB-Ordnance agreement in late 1917 was substantial indeed.

Another difficulty caused by American entry to the war was that supplies of critical war materials, hitherto readily obtainable in the United States, were now needed by America's industries as they geared up for war production. Steel available for export to Canada, for example, became scarce. To resolve such scarcities, Ottawa set up a Canadian War Mission in Washington, and it worked diligently to see that Canada got its fair share of scarce supplies. At the same time, the government created controllers to allocate scarce resources, in part an effort to demonstrate to Washington that Canadians were not wasting materials any more than Americans. In effect, Canada became a region to be treated in Washington much like the Midwest or the South, and Canadians argued successfully that the Allied war effort made it essential for scarce materials to be allocated where they could be most efficiently used.[33] That meant that Canada had to get its fair share. The *Financial Post* summed it all up in one headline in December 1917: 'Canada's Prosperity to Depend on Close Cooperation in Aims and Objects with the United States.'[34]

Inevitably there were difficulties in working out the modalities of the new situation. In February 1918 Prime Minister Robert Borden went to see President Woodrow Wilson. Borden's object was to get the American leader to resist the bureaucratic efforts in the u.s. capital to have American resources and war orders directed to American factories. Borden succeeded, for Wilson agreed that orders and supplies could continue to flow northwards. As the prime minister wrote expansively, Wilson had 'expressed the view that the resources of the two countries should be pooled in the most effective co-operation and that the boundary line had little or no significance in considering or dealing with these vital questions.'[35]

What, however, did all this mean? London's inability to pay in full for the goods it received from Canada was understandable, and a case can be made that as a British dominion involved in the war, Canada had to help its mother country to the full. Few would quarrel strenuously with that proposition. But Britain's terrible shortage of American dollars was such that, in order to raise money, Canada had to go to the u.s. market and had, as a result, to increase its dependency on the Americans. Sir Thomas White had to strike a special arrangement with the u.s. government so he could borrow in New York, and British negotiators had to plead on Ottawa's behalf for extra American dollars. Moreover, the fall in British war orders meant that the Imperial Munitions Board and the Canadian government believed that they had to turn to the u.s. War Department for relief so that Canadian munitions production could continue at a high level.

The ironies here are delicious. Canada had exerted itself to help the mother country in its hour of need and, as a result, had slid into a huge trade deficit with the United States. The leader of the anti-reciprocity Toronto Eighteen had been forced to ask the secretary of the u.s. Treasury for favours. Sir Joseph Flavelle had looked for contracts from the War Department to make up for shortfalls in British orders. And, most ironic of all, Sir Robert

Borden had tried to win Woodrow Wilson's agreement in a summit meeting to continue American war orders in Canadian factories. The architects of the 'No Truck or Trade with the Yankees' campaign of 1911 had just seven years later to plead for special treatment in Washington. Borden's relief when Wilson told him that the border should cease to exist for war purposes was palpable.

No one should doubt that it was War exigency that forced these moves on Borden, White, Flavelle, and Canada, though the necessity of keeping up munitions orders with an election in the offing was also a major factor. Essentially, it was the economic weakness of Great Britain that made the negotiations a necessity.

These moves were crucial in economic terms, but their symbolism is even more important. They represented the beginning of the shift in economic power from Britain to the United States, from The City to Wall Street, as well as Canada's increasing dependence on the United States. There were other indicators of that growing dependence too. In 1900, American foreign investment in Canada amounted only to 14 per cent of the total while British investment was 85 per cent. In 1914, the figures were 23 and 72 per cent, respectively; but by 1918, American investment had risen to 36 per cent of the total and British investment had declined to 60 per cent. Nor was the British decline in economic influence in Canada arrested by the Armistice; by 1922 American investment for the first time exceeded British.[36] Similarly, Canadian exports to the United States, in 1901 less than half those to Britain, grew rapidly until in 1918 they were four-fifths of a much larger total going to England. Imports showed even more dramatic change. In 1901 imports from the United Kingdom were $42 million and from the United States, $110 million. In 1918, however, imports from the south were ten times those from Great Britain.[37] Although there was a certain reversion towards a more normal trading pattern in the postwar years, Canada had, during the Great War, shifted out of the British economic orbit and towards, if not yet completely into, the American.

No one has ever suggested that Sir Robert Borden, Sir Thomas White, and Sir Joseph Flavelle deliberately sold Canada out when they turned to the United States for help as British strength waned in 1916, 1917, and 1918. Nor would I. Borden had to do what he did to keep the Canadian war effort and economy going – and to ensure his re-election in 1917. Still, this nationalist-imperialist prime minister might have given some thought to the long-term implications of his and his government's actions. That, after all, is what the critics of Mackenzie King's very similar activities during the Second World War would say, only in far harsher terms.

2

Staring
into
the Abyss

'HISTORY REPEATS ITSELF.' That is a popular view of the past, but it is not, I suspect, a view shared by most historians. The differences in personalities, in context, in subtleties and shadings usually combine to persuade historians that the crisis of one decade or century is different in class and kind from that of another. But, sometimes, history really does seem to repeat itself.

In the First World War, as we have seen, the United Kingdom's weakened financial condition led Whitehall to pressure Canada to turn to the United States to raise money. At the same time, Britain proved unable or unwilling to take all the food and munitions produced by Canada unless Ottawa picked up a greater share of the costs, and the Canadian government had little choice other than to agree. In an effort, both politically and economically inspired, to keep nunitions factories working at full blast in Canada, the Imperial Munitions Board, a Canadian-operated imperial procurement and production agency, actively sought contracts from the U.S. War Department. At the same time, other arms of the Canadian government lobbied in Washington to get their share of scarce raw materials. The net effect of the First World War on Canadian-American relations was to strengthen the links across the border and to increase the number and complexity of the ties of economics, politics, and sentiment that bound the two North American nations together. The defeat of reciprocity in the 1911 election, therefore, seemed only a temporary check, one virtually nullified by the greater necessity of wartime integration and cooperation.

It should have been no surprise, then, that Canada entered the 1920s with Conservative Prime Minister Arthur Meighen urging Britain to seek an accommodation with the United States and not to renew the Angle-Japanese Alliance.[1] Nor was it a surprise that Canada welcomed more investment from the United States while, despite repeated efforts by the Liberal governments of Mackenzie King to enhance trade with the United Kingdom, its commerce with its neighbour continued to increase.[2] The

Great Depression and the massive increases in the American tariff put in place by a protectionist Congress and then matched by Canadian governments, however, temporarily cut into Canadian-American trade.

While these restrictions led many Canadians to look overseas with renewed imperial fervour, some Britons nonetheless feared for Canada's survival as a British nation in the face of the power of the United States. One example of the first tendency was Harry Stevens, soon to be minister of trade and commerce in R.B. Bennett's government, who told the voters in 1930 that 'My ambition for Canada is that she may become a unit of the Empire and concerned not with a few petty tariff items, but with all the great problems confronting the Home Government.' No worse fate could have befallen Canadians! In contrast, Leo Amery, the dominions secretary in 1928, returned from a trip to Canada worried that 'the din and glare of the great American orchestra' might drown out Canada. His hopes were bolstered, however, by the conviction that there was 'no deeper fundamental instinct of the Canadian national character than dislike of the United States as belonging to an inferior political civilisation.'[3] For their part, officials of the United States government, as Peter Kasurak has noted, began 'from a single point of view in the area of Canadian affairs – fear that Britain was forging its Empire into an international colossus which would dominate world trade.'[4] To Washington, that fear seemed to be realized after the Ottawa Conference of 1932.[5]

But not even the Imperial Economic Conference and the imperial preferences agreed on at Ottawa could truly reverse the historic trend towards North American continentalism that had accelerated during the Great War. The two 'hermit kingdoms,' to use Charles Stacey's phrase uttered from this platform a dozen years ago,[6] had a great deal in common in an era when British trade as a percentage of world trade continued its decline and Britain's overall military power ebbed. Mackenzie King had begun the transformation of the empire into the Commonwealth during the Chanak affair of 1922 and at the Imperial Conference of 1923, where 'the decisive nature of the English defeat at Mackenzie King's hands' was nothing less than a 'surrender, which changed the course of the history of the empire.'[7] Those apocalyptic phrases were the considered judgment of Correlli Barnett, 'the Jeremiah of British historians,' or so Noel Annan has recently called him.[8] They sound very similar in tone to the words of Donald Creighton, the Jeremiah of Canadian historians, who wrote that King, 'a stocky barrel-like figure, with an audible wheeze when in full voice,' was no 'bulky St. George confronting a slavering imperial dragon.' He was 'a citizen of North America ... determined to destroy' the Commonwealth.[9]

When Mackenzie King came back to power in the middle of the Great Depression in 1935, the Ottawa agreements had demonstrably not restored Canada's economic health. Prime Minister Bennett had seemingly recognized the failure of the imperial initiative by launching his own somewhat desultory efforts to strike a trade agreement with Washington, but his attempt at an accommodation with the United States could not come to fruition before the voters eagerly dispensed with the Tory government's services.[10] It fell to the new prime minister, choosing what he described to the United States minister in Canada as 'the American road,' to negotiate that trade agreement with the Roosevelt administration.[11] Mackenzie King reinforced it with another trade pact with the United States three years later.[12] Simultaneously, King and his advisers in the Department of External Affairs looked with dismay at the wide-ranging rivalry between London and Washington, most pronounced in the Pacific where the two English-speaking powers jostled for economic and political dominance with each other and an aggressive Japan. Conflict between Canada's mother country and its nearest neighbour held out only the prospect of terrible divisiveness in Canada.[13] Nonetheless, the prime minister gladly accepted and immediately reciprocated President Franklin Roosevelt's assurances, delivered at Queen's University in Kingston on 18 August 1938, 'that the people of the United States will not stand idly by' if Canada were ever threatened.[14] That guarantee had to be called upon just two years later.

By 1939, as the Nazis prepared to plunge Europe into the war that was to ensure America's half century of world economic hegemony, u.s. companies and investors and the American market had already established their pre-eminence in Canada. The United States provided 60 per cent of the foreign capital invested in Canada while British sources put up only 36 per cent. In 1914 the figures had been 23 and 72 per cent, respectively. In terms of Canadian exports, shipments to the United States in 1939 exceeded those to Britain by 20 per cent; in 1914 exports to Britain had been 10 per cent higher than those to the United States. Similarly, in 1914 Canada had imported three times as much from the United States as from the United Kingdom; in 1939 Canada imported four times as much.[15] The years of the Great War had provided the impetus for Canada's shift from the British to the American economic sphere.

During the Second World War, the events of the Great War were repeated with a stunning similarity. To be sure, different men from different political parties were in charge in Canada. Mackenzie King, that most unadmired of Canadian leaders, was at the helm in Ottawa, and his attitudes and prejudices were certainly far different from those of Sir Robert Borden.

Ramsay Cook predicted almost two decades ago that King was certain to become the subject of a book of readings for students under the title 'Mackenzie King: Hero or Fink?' Cook knew that the fink side of the debate would be easy to document. He suggested that King had become the central figure in the Canadian mythology, the most convenient one of all, because he was the 'cause of all our failings,' including the decline and fall of the British Empire in Canada.[16] Cook was certainly correct in assessing the little man's place, and few have yet come forward to argue that Mackenzie King was a great Canadian hero. Charles Stacey, in the last words of his Joanne Goodman lectures in 1976, however, did say – and I expect he was only half-jesting – that he would 'not be altogether surprised if he turned up, one of these days, as the patron saint of the new nationalism.'[17] Still, King is difficult to elevate to sainthood. Even (or especially) those who observed or worked intimately with him had scant admiration for him. Tom Blacklock, a Press Gallery member in the 1920s, complained that King was 'such a pompous ass that an orang-outang that would flatter him could choose its own reward.'[18] Leonard Brockington wrote speeches for King for a time during the early years of the Second World War, and when he quit in exasperation he told a friend that he was 'sick and tired of being mid-wife to an intellectual virgin.'[19] Senator Norman Lambert ran elections for the Liberal leader, and Mackenzie King gratefully elevated him to the Upper Chamber. Nonetheless, Lambert told Grant Dexter of the *Winnipeg Free Press* that 'he simply can't stand the worm at close quarters – bad breath, a fetid, unhealthy, sinister atmosphere like living close to some filthy object ... But,' the senator added, 'get off a piece and he looks better and better.'[20]

That last comment on Mackenzie King I have always thought the nearly definitive one. Up close, there was little that was admirable about the Liberal leader, much that was slippery and sleazy. But acquire some distance, get off a piece, as Lambert said, and the dumpy little laird of Kingsmere – and Canada – began to look not unlike a giant. To bring us back to Earth, I might point out that the fine Canadian novelist Hugh Hood has his main character in *The Swing in the Garden* note, 'I think always of W.C. Fields when I think of Mackenzie King.'[21] That may be *the* definitive description.

I have no intention of trying to paint Mackenzie King as a superhero here, though, despite years of reading Donald Creighton and W.L. Morton, I cannot yet bring myself to see him as a filthy object or even as a fink. For me, the crucial factor in assessing the common charge that Mackenzie King sold us out to the Americans is that the prime minister during the Second World War faced similar, but greater, problems to those Sir Robert Borden had had to confront a quarter century before. But though he had more resources at his disposal than his predecessor in the Prime Minister's office, King had no greater freedom of action when British military and economic weakness forced his country into grave difficulties. When it came to directing the weak corner of the North Atlantic Triangle in its efforts to stay safe and secure in a world suddenly unstable, King, much like Borden before him, had to turn to the United States for assistance.

One major factor was different in the Second World War. In the Great War, Britain and France lost battles but they did not suffer catastrophic defeats that placed their survival as nation-states at stake. In May and June 1940, of course, Hitler's astonishingly effective armies defeated Britain and France in the Low Countries and in France, the French capitulated, and the British Army, without equipment, found its way home thanks only to a miracle at Dunkirk.

For Canada in that terrible summer of defeat and despair, the changes in the military balance of power were catastrophic. The country had gone to war with the idea that it could fight as a junior partner with 'limited liability.' The government had hoped that its war effort could be small, balanced, and relatively cheap, and Quebec and the country had been promised that there would be no conscription for overseas service. Now, the planning of late 1939 had to be scrapped. Canada, with its population of eleven million and suddenly Britain's ranking ally, was in the war to the utmost – except for conscription, which was still politically unacceptable. Moreover, a huge proportion of this country's under-equipped and partially trained air, army, and naval forces was already in the United Kingdom, and if – or when – Britain fell they were certain to be completely lost. The Royal Navy had its hands full in trying to protect home waters and block the expected Nazi invasion. The aircraft necessary to operate the centrepiece of the Canadian war effort, the British Commonwealth Air Training Plan, had been scheduled to come from Great Britain, but now would not arrive. If Britain fell and, especially, if the Royal Navy passed into German hands, Canada was likely to be subject to Nazi attack.[22] Britain's military weakness in July and August 1940 was exposed for all to see; so too was Canada's.[23]

The military weakness of the United States was also apparent, but there can be no doubt that President Franklin Roosevelt's country was the only hope of the Allies – and of Canada. Many in Canada recognized this truth in the days after Dunkirk, and they realized the new obligations this would force on the dominion. Donald Creighton, writing years later, noted that for many Canadians – and he had his despised colleague Frank Underhill in mind – the war's course 'hastened the growth' of Canada's 'new North American nationality by proving that ... Great Britain ... could no longer act as Canada's main defence against danger from abroad.'[24]

At the time, the bureaucratic response to the new state of affairs came from Hugh Keenleyside of the Department of External Affairs, who set out the fullest statement of the likely Canadian situation as France surrendered to Hitler. It was improbable, he wrote, that the United States would protect Canada without 'demanding a measure of active cooperation in return. It is a reasonable expectation that the United States will expect, and if necessary demand, Canadian assistance in the defence of this continent and this Hemisphere.' Canada, he noted, would feel some obligation to participate; 'thus the negotiation of a specific offensive-defensive alliance is likely to become inevitable.'[25]

President Roosevelt himself was thinking along these lines. In

August, Loring Christie, the Canadian minister in Washington, reported to Mackenzie King that the president 'had been thinking of proposing to you to send to Ottawa 3 staff officers ... to discuss defence problems ... He had in mind their surveying [the] situation from [the] Bay of Fundy around to the Gulf of St. Lawrence. They might explore [the] question of base facilities for United States use.'[26] But on 16 August Roosevelt asked King to meet him at Ogdensburg, NY, the next day to discuss 'the matter of [the] mutual defence of our coasts on the Atlantic.'[27]

What the president wanted was the creation of a Permanent Joint Board on Defence with equal representation from each country and a mandate limited to the study of common defence problems and the making of recommendations to both governments on how to resolve them. Delighted at the prospect of forging a military alliance with the United States, King queried only Roosevelt's desire that the board be 'permanent.' 'I said I was not questioning the wisdom of it,' King noted, 'but was anxious to get what he had in mind.' According to King's diary, Roosevelt replied that he wanted 'to help secure the continent for the future.'[28] The Canadian leader sometimes suffered from 'the idea,' in the superb Australian novelist Thomas Keneally's phrase, 'that the only empire you need to suspect is the British.'[29] Mackenzie King probably ought to have asked whose empire and whose future, but in August 1940 that question was virtually impossible even to raise – when the fear was that it might be Adolf Hitler's empire and Germany's future if no action were taken.

The decision to create the PJBD was an important one. The board sprang into existence within two weeks and began surveying defences on both the Atlantic and the Pacific coasts. A Joint Canadian-United States Basic Defence Plan, produced by the board's military members, aimed to meet the situation that would arise if Britain were overrun. In that event, strategic control of Canadian forces was to pass to the United States. A second plan, produced in the spring of 1941 and called ABC-22, looked at Canadian-American cooperation in a war in which the United States was actively engaged on the side of the Allies. The Americans again sought strategic control of Canadian forces and to integrate the Canadian east and west coast regions directly into their military commands. It was one thing to agree to American military direction in a war that saw North America standing virtually alone; it was another thing entirely in a war where Britain remained unoccupied and the United States was a partner. 'The American officers,' to use Keneally again, 'listened ... with that omnivorous American politeness ... we poor hayseeds would come to know so well and mistrust, perhaps, not enough.'[30] Nonetheless, Canada refused to accept Washington's aims for ABC-22 and won its point, thereby demonstrating that Mackenzie King's government could and would fight for its freedom of action.[31] Whether such independence could have survived a German or Japanese invasion happily never had to be tested.

The significance of the PJBD in its context of August 1940 was that a still-neutral United States had struck an alliance with Canada, a belligerent power. That had to be seen as a gain for Britain – and for Canada, too. Important as that was for the war, the true meaning of the Ogdensburg meeting was that it marked Canada's definitive move from the British military sphere to the American. The British had lost whatever capacity they might have had to defend Canada, and in August 1940 their ability even to defend the British Isles successfully was very much in doubt.[32] In the circumstances, Canada had no choice at all. Canada had to seek help where help was to be found, and that meant Washington.

Few people truly realized the significance of the Permanent Joint Board on Defence and the Ogdensburg Agreement that had created it in the summer of 1940. Some Conservatives grumbled at Mackenzie King's actions, former Prime Minister Arthur Meighen being the most caustic. He had noted that 'I lost my breakfast when I read the account this morning and gazed on the disgusting picture of these potentates' – that is, King and Roosevelt – 'posing like monkeys in the very middle of the blackest crisis of this Empire.'[33] Most Tories and almost all the Canadian press showed more sense.[34]

The one critic who shook Mackenzie King, however, was Winston Churchill. The new British prime minister, in office only since 10 May 1940, had replied to King's telegram on the Ogdensburg meeting by stating 'there may be two opinions on some of the points mentioned. Supposing Mr. Hitler cannot invade us ... all these transactions will be judged in a mood different to that prevailing while the issue still hangs in the balance.'[35] Churchill, disgustedly seeing Canada scurrying for shelter under the eagle's wing, evidently realized that a major shift had occurred. What he would have had Canada do, what he would have done differently had he been Canadian prime minister, was never stated. Certainly he failed to recognize that with its security now guaranteed by the United States, Canada could send every man and weapon possible to defend Britain, something it dutifully and willingly did.

As for me, no matter how often I try to appraise the situation, I cannot see any other option for Mackenzie King. The issue potentially was the survival of the Canadian nation in face of an apparently defeated Great Britain and a victorious Nazi Germany. King did what he had to do to secure Canada's security. The reason Mackenzie King had to strike his arrangement with Roosevelt was the military weakness of Great Britain in the summer of 1940.[36]

The immediate result of the Ogdensburg Agreement was wholly beneficial to Canada and Canadian interests. But we can see now that the long-term implications included the construction of major American installations and the presence in substantial numbers of American troops in the Canadian Northwest from 1942,[37] the 1947 military agreement with the United States that continued joint defence cooperation, the North American Air Defence Agreement of 1957–8, and eventually even Cruise missile testing and the possibility of Star Wars installations in the Canadian North.

Many Canadians may be less than happy with the way matters turned out. In his *Lament for a Nation*, George Grant wrote:

> In 1940, it was necessary for Canada to throw in her lot with continental defence. The whole of Eurasia might have fallen into the hands of Germany and Japan. The British Empire was collapsing once and for all as an international force. Canada and the United States of America had to be unequivocally united for the defence of this hemisphere. But it is surprising how little the politicians and officials seem to have realized that this new situation would have to be manipulated with great wisdom if any Canadian independence was to survive. Perhaps nothing could have been done; perhaps the collapse of nineteenth-century Europe automatically entailed the collapse of Canada. Nonetheless, it is extraordinary that King and his associates in External Affairs did not seem to recognize the perilous situation that the new circumstances entailed. In all eras, wise politicians have to play a balancing game. How little the American alliance was balanced by any defence of national independence.![38]

Much of Grant's assessment is correct. Certainly, Canada had no choice in August 1940 in the situation in which it found itself. But to me, Mackenzie King's actions in August 1940 were an attempt to protect Canadian independence – and ensure Canada's survival – in a world that had been turned upside down in a few months by the defeat of Britain and France. Grant, writing a quarter century after the event, does not say what King might have done after Ogdensburg to achieve a balance to the American alliance. Nor did Churchill in 1940. In the remainder of this essay, I will try to show how King successfully struggled to preserve at least a measure of financial independence for Canada.

Those who believe, like George Grant and Donald Creighton, that the Ogdensburg Agreement and its aftermath were a virtual sell-out to the United States have an obligation to offer an alternative vision. If there was 'a forked road' in August 1940 and if Canada went in the wrong direction, where might the other road have led? What should Mackenzie King and his government have done that they did not do? I await the response.

The Ogdensburg Agreement had secured Canada's physical defences, but it had done nothing to resolve the country's economic difficulties. As in the Great War, the problem came about because Canada was caught between a strong United States and its desire to help an economically weak Great Britain. Indeed, Britain was weak. The ambassador in Washington, Lord Lothian, summed it up when he told a group of reporters: 'Boys, Britain's broke. It's your money we want.'[39] It was soon to be Canada's money that London wanted too.

Britain had begun the war in 1939 convinced that purchases had to be switched away from North America to conserve scarce dollar exchange. That laudable goal threatened Canadian tobacco, fruit, and wheat exports and provoked extraordinary outrage in Ottawa and threats that such a policy might hurt what Mackenzie King delicately called 'our ability to render assistance.' Similarly, British munitions orders in the Phoney War months were less than expected; that too angered the King government. But the same German victories that forced Canada to seek assistance to the south also obliged London to look to Canada for more – more money, more food, more munitions, more of everything.[40]

By February 1941, therefore, the Department of Finance in Ottawa estimated that the British deficit with Canada was $795 million, an amount that had been covered by transfers of gold, debt repatriation, and a large sterling accumulation in London.[41] Ottawa also predicted that war expenditures for the year would amount to $1.4 billion and that $433 million was needed for civil expenditure. A further $400 million would be required to repatriate additional Canadian securities held in Britain, in effect a way of giving Britain additional Canadian dollars with which to pay for the goods it bought in Canada. At the same time, the mandarins in Finance estimated that the provincial and municipal governments would spend $575 million for a total governmental expenditure of almost half Canada's Gross National Income.[42] Could the country function, they asked, if half of all production were devoted to government operations?

Historically, Canada's economic position had depended on the maintenance of a 'bilateral unbalance within a balanced "North Atlantic Triangle."'[43] That meant, in effect, that our chronic trade deficit with the United States was covered by a surplus with Britain. Pounds earned in London were readily converted to American dollars, and thus the bills could be paid. But now sterling was inconvertible, and as Canada built up large balances in London, these could no longer be used to cover the trade deficit with the United States.

Compounding the problem was that as Canada strained to produce greater quantities of war material and food for Britain, more components and raw materials had to be imported from the United States. Every time, for example, that a truck, built in Canada by General Motors or Ford, went to Britain, it contained an imported engine, specialty steels, and a variety of parts brought in from south of the border. Almost a third of the value of a tank, ship, or artillery piece had to be imported. The result was a classic squeeze. Canadian goods went to Great Britain where the British could pay for them only in sterling, which was of little use to Canada outside the British Isles (though we could buy New Zealand lamb or Malayan tin, for example, with it). In effect, Canada was financing the British trade deficit. But at the same time and as a result of war production for Britain, Canadian imports from the United States were expanding rapidly, far more so than exports to the United States. The result was a huge trade deficit with the United States, one that grew worse the more Canada tried to help Britain. In April 1941 Ottawa's estimates of the deficit for that fiscal year were $478 million; by June, officials argued that imports from the United States had risen by $400 million a year while exports to the south had increased by only half that sum.[44]

Canada had been trying to grapple with this problem for some time. Efforts had been made since September 1939 to control foreign exchange, to promote Canada as a tourist mecca for Americans ('Ski in a country at war,' the advertisements could have said), and by devaluing the dollar to 90 cents U.S. to restrict imports from and encourage export sales to the United States. Each measure had some positive results, but together they amounted to very little against the flood of components pouring over the border for an expanding war industry. Soon, Ottawa slapped stringent controls on the U.S. dollars Canadian travellers could acquire, and a wide range of import prohibitions were put in place in December 1940 on unnecessary imports. Those measures, strong enough to anger the American government and American exporters, also failed completely to reverse the steady growth in the deficit with the United States.[45]

What else remained? A loan from the United States government? O.D. Skelton, the undersecretary of state for external affairs until his death in January 1941, told Pierrepont Moffat, the very able American minister in Canada, that 'it would be disastrous to face a future of making heavy interest payments to the United States year after year in perpetuity, or alternatively having a war debt controversy.'[46] Canada was physically too close to the United States to owe debt directly to Washington, or so Skelton and his colleagues in the Ottawa mandarinate believed. What then? Could Canadian investments in the United States, estimated at $275 million to $1 billion in worth, be sold off to raise American dollars? They could, but those investments cushioned Canada from the strain of her foreign indebtedness, and there were obvious

political problems in forcing private investors to sell their holdings at wartime fire-sale prices.[47] That was not a feasible route
for the Mackenzie King government.

At this point, the situation altered dramatically. The United
States Congress accepted President Roosevelt's proposal for Lend-
Lease, a scheme to permit the United States to give the Allies
war materiel effectively free of monetary cost, though there were
political costs of which the British were all too aware.[48] The
initial appropriation accompanying the bill was $7 billion. This
was, as Churchill called it, 'the most unsordid act,' an extraordinarily generous step by the still-neutral United States. But Lend-
Lease posed terrible problems for Ottawa. First, the Canadian
government did not want to take charity from the United States –
'the psychological risk,' two historians noted, 'of becoming a
pensioner of the United States was too great.'[49] Second, if Britain
could get war materiel from the United States free of charge,
what was to happen to the orders it had placed in Canada and
for which it had to pay, even if only with inconvertible sterling?
C.D. Howe, presiding over Canada's war production as the minister of munitions and supply, told the Cabinet War Committee
that he was 'gravely concerned' that those orders might be shifted
to the United States.[50] If that happened, what would the impact
be on Canada's war employment and wartime prosperity? It was
the spring of 1917 all over again, and history repeated itself.

The British characteristically and quickly saw the advantages
offered by the situation and began to press Canada. Although
junior ministers in Churchill's cabinet bemoaned what they saw
as Canada's accelerating drift out of the empire,[51] the hard-
headed officials at the Treasury knew what they wanted. Cut
purchases of non-essential goods in the United States, Ottawa
was told. Accept Lend-Lease. Sell off Canadian securities held
in the United States. Such a regimen meant higher taxes and
inflation for the Canadians, the British knew, but as the Treasury officials said, 'It is as much in their interests as in ours to act

along these lines, seeing that our only alternative, if we are unable to pay for our orders in Canada, is to place them instead in the United States in cases in which we should be able to obtain the goods under the "Lease and Lend" Act.'[52]

Thus Canada's problem. Some way had to be found to keep the British orders, so essential for wartime prosperity, without selling the country lock, stock, and barrel to the United States. Though the Liberal government faced no immediate election, as had Borden in 1917 in similar circumstances, the retention of prosperity was every bit as much a political necessity. At the same time, and again the parallel with Sir Thomas White's refusal to borrow from the u.s. government is clear, the King government was adamant in its refusal to take Lend-Lease. That was little better than a loan and, while relations with Franklin Roosevelt's Washington were very good, no one wanted to be quite so indebted to the great nation with which Canada shared the continent. The Americans, as Clifford Clark, deputy minister of finance, noted fearfully, might later drive a very hard bargain on tariffs.[53] Nonetheless, Canada's trade with the United States somehow had to be brought into balance.

The ideal solution, as Canadian officials came to realize in the spring of 1941, was an arrangement that would see the United States increase its purchases in Canada and, in addition, supply the components and raw materials Canada needed to produce munitions for the United Kingdom. Those components could be charged to Britain's Lend-Lease account, a clever device that could let Canada keep its war economy going at full blast without bankrupting itself in the process. In the meantime, desperate to ensure the continuation of orders in Canada, Ottawa agreed to finance the British deficit with Canada.[54] That was again a repetition of the events of 1917. Though there is no sign in the files that anyone realized this parallel, so too was the Canadian proposal to the United States.

The Hyde Park Declaration, signed by Mackenzie King and Franklin Roosevelt on 'a grand Sunday' in April, put the seal on the Canadian proposal. The United States agreed to spend $200–300 million more in Canada, largely for raw materials and aluminum. 'Why not buy from Canada as much as Canada is buying from the United States,' Mackenzie King said he had told the president, '– just balance the accounts. Roosevelt thought this was a swell idea.'[55] In addition, the president agreed that Britain's Lend-Lease account could be charged with the materials and components Canada needed to produce munitions for export.[56] That too dealt the trade deficit a mighty blow.

The declaration signed at Hyde Park was a splendid achievement for Canada. Howe told Mackenzie King that he was 'the greatest negotiator the country had or something about being the world's best negotiator,' the prime minister recorded.[57] Howe soon created War Supplies Limited, a crown corporation with E.P. Taylor as its head, to sell Canadian-manufactured war equipment and raw materials in the United States.[58]

The Hyde Park Declaration allowed Canada to do its utmost for Britain without fear of financial collapse. Most important, King had won Roosevelt's agreement without having to give up anything tangible – in the short-run. Unlike Great Britain, Canada was not obliged to sell off its investments prior to receiving u.s. aid; nor was Canada to be required to take Lend-Lease, both measures that the government sought to avoid.[59] Knowing that the desperate plight of the British had forced him to seek assistance for Canada from the United States, Mackenzie King had secured that help on the very best terms. For his part, Roosevelt could agree to King's proposals (incidentally, entirely on his own without any consultation with Congress or the State Department) because they cost the United States almost nothing, because he was friendly to Canada, and because he considered that his country's long-term interests would be best served by having an amicable and prosperous Canada on his northern border, a nation tightly linked to the United States. Undoubtedly, Roosevelt was correct. He served his country's interests well.

In retrospect, however, we can see that the inextricable linkages created or strengthened by the Second World War were the key long-term results of the 1941 agreement. The Hyde Park Declaration effectively wiped out the border for war purposes, allowing raw materials to pour south while munitions components came north. To help the war effort, to produce the goods for a desperate Great Britain, Mackenzie King's Canada tied itself to the United States for the war's duration. There is no point in complaining about this almost a half century later. The Hyde Park Declaration was one of many actions that were necessary to win the war against Hitler, and everything done to further that end was proper and right. But neither is there any point in blinking at the facts. Canada tied itself to the United States in 1941, just as it had done in 1917, because Britain was economically weak. That weakness forced Canada to look to Washington for assistance, and the Americans provided it, freely and willingly. It served Washington's interests; it served Canada's immediate interests; above all, it served the cause of victory.

The short-term results of the Hyde Park Declaration were much as the Canadian government had hoped. American purchases in Canada rose rapidly, and Canada's dollar shortage came to an end in 1942; indeed, the next year controls had to be put in place to prevent Canada's holdings of u.s. dollars from growing too large. The wartime prosperity that Hyde Park solidified was such that in 1942 Canada could offer Great Britain a gift of $1 billion, and the next year Canada created a Mutual Aid program that eventually gave Britain an additional $2 billion in munitions and foodstuffs. The total of Canadian aid to Great Britain during the war was $3.468 billion[60] – and a billion then was really worth a billion. That was help to a valued ally and friend, of course, just as much as it was an investment in continued high employment at home. As an official in the Dominions Office in London noted, 'Per head of population the Canadian gifts will cost Canada about five times what lend lease costs the United States. Canada's income tax is already as high as ours; it may have to go higher ... Canada is devoting as large a proportion of her national income to defence expenditure as any other country; in no other country is the proportion of defence expenditure which is given away in the form of free supplies anywhere near so high as in Canada.'[61] The war had cost Canada about $18 billion, and almost one-fifth of that staggering total was given to Britain in the form of gifts. That Canada could offer such assistance freely was the best proof possible that Mackenzie King's policy in 1941 had been correct and successful.

Still, there can be no doubt that the Hyde Park Declaration reinforced the trends that had begun to take form during the Great War. Some of those were psychological. Two bureaucrats who dealt with the United States regularly during the war had gushed fellowship in an article they published in the *Canadian Journal of Economics and Political Science* at the end of the war. 'There has been the open exchange of confidence between the Americans and Canadians, the warm welcome, the freedom from formality, the plain speaking and the all-pervading friendship,' Sydney Pierce and A.F.W. Plumptre wrote. This was the result of 'our common background of language and culture, and to the close trade and industrial relationship: in part it is due to the fact that our approach to problems is similar.'[62] That was all true, too.

Other trends were financial and commercial. By 1945 American investment had risen to 70 per cent of the total foreign capital invested in Canada. Exports to the United States were more than three times what they had been in 1939 and were 25 per cent greater than war-swollen Canadian exports to Britain. Imports from the United States were now ten times those from Britain.[63] The war undoubtedly had distorted Canada's trade figures, but the direction was clear and it would be confirmed by the events of the reconstruction period.

By 1945 Canada was part and parcel of the continental economy. It was a two-way North American street now, and the North Atlantic Triangle, if it still existed at all, was a casualty of the world wars. Despite this, as we shall see in the concluding essay, the Canadian government tried desperately, if unsuccessfully, to restore the traditional balance in the postwar years.

3

Over the Edge

IN THE BROADWAY MUSICAL *Pal Joey*, one of the main characters takes off her clothes in a bump-and-grind routine. In her song, the amateur ecdysiast says, 'I was reading Schopenhauer last night, and I think that Schopenhauer is right.' Well, I was reading Hegel last night, and I think that Hegel is right. Especially when he said, 'What experience and history teach is this – that people and governments never have learned anything from history, or acted on principles deduced from it.' Regrettably, Hegel was probably correct, and it may be that there is no better example than the efforts of the Canadian government to help its struggling mother country, Great Britain, in the years after the Second World War.

Surely this country's government ought to have learned from experience. In the Great War, the British in their financial desperation and exhaustion had pressed Canada to raise money in the United States and encouraged the forgoing of economic links across the border so that Canadian industry might better serve the British and Allied war effort. In the Second World War, British military weakness obliged Canada to ensure its national security by striking a military alliance with the United States. British financial weakness similarly demanded that Canada find some way of increasing its exports of raw materials to the United States to cover the trade deficit resulting from the import of munitions components necessary so that Canada could support Great Britain. The Hyde Park Declaration of April 1941 resolved Canada's economic problems, just as the Ogdensburg Agreement of 1940 had solved her military security problems. But the net result was that Canada and the United States emerged from the Second World War more closely linked than ever.

Surely there could not be a third instance in which Britain's weakness would force Canada to the south? In fact, as we shall see, the Mackenzie King government's efforts to help Britain and to keep up Anglo-Canadian trade led to precisely this outcome. Britain's economic weakness drove Canada to Washington yet again, and for a third time in just three decades the United States freely offered the requested assistance. After that happy event, Canada entered a long era of unprecedented prosperity, enjoying a standard of living undreamed of before the start of the 1939 war. All that had been sacrificed to achieve this prolonged boom was Canada's chance of economic and military independence.

When he considered the postwar period in his *The Forked Road: Canada 1939–1957*, Donald Creighton wrote that Liberal prime ministers Mackenzie King and Louis St Laurent 'stubbornly continued to act as if they still cherished the senile delusion that freedom from British control was alone necessary to ensure Canadian autonomy, and that independence in a continent dominated by the United States was an easy and effortless business which had no need of constant attention and protective care.'[1] That, I have to say, is a wholly uninformed and inaccurate assessment, as incorrect as Creighton's overview of Canadian history with which I began this series of essays.

Nor is James Laxer's 'Liberal sell-out' interpretation of what happened any more complete. In his most recent book, *Decline of the Superpowers*, Laxer notes that Canada was at a crossroads in 1945. 'For the Liberal government of Mackenzie King,' he says, 'it was natural enough to base post-war economic policy on still closer ties with the United States.' Most especially, 'it was American investment that would guarantee takeoff. u.s. investment poured into the manufacturing and resource sectors of the Canadian economy.'[2] Some of that is true, but Laxer seems completely unaware of the reasons Canada had to choose the American road. The reasons, almost as much as the result, are what matter.

The world in 1945 was in ruins. Britain, Europe, and Asia had been destroyed by six years of war. Their housing stock was bombed into rubble, much of their industrial plant was levelled or just plain worn-out, and their men, women, and children were dead or dying of malnutrition and disease. Only two nations had emerged from the Second World War stronger economically, politically, and militarily than when they entered it, Canada and the United States. Both North American nations were committed and idealistic, Canadians probably more so than Americans, though Canada, of course, had far less strength than its super-power neighbour. Like the Americans, Canada's government and almost all her businessmen wanted to see a world that traded freely on a multilateral basis. Such a situation, replacing the prewar world of high tariffs, was in Canada's interest, one that would allow us to capitalize on our strengths, our ability to produce, and the advantage we had after 1945 of having goods for sale in what was expected to be a seller's market.

But what country could buy what Canada had to sell? The world was starving and impoverished, and few nations had the dollars to pay us for our food and manufactured goods. Unless we found buyers, Canadian workers and farmers might find themselves on the pogey once more. The choice in 1945 seemed to be either to give aid to our traditional trading partners in Britain and Europe or to face massive unemployment at home. The Canadian government sensibly chose to offer aid.

The result was an unprecedented and generous program that saw Canada provide $2.2 billion in loans and credits to Britain and the Western European nations in the years immediately after the war. Our object was twofold: idealistically to help recon-struct and rehabilitate a ravaged world and, out of self-interest, to keep up Canadian exports and prosperity. The United States did much the same although, in proportionate terms, Canada's assistance was greater. But then our dependence on trade was also greater. To cite only a few examples, Britain took almost all of Canada's exports of eggs, bacon, and canned salmon, and a high proportion of exports of wheat, newsprint, and timber. If the British could not pay for these goods, where was Canada to sell them?

The major part of the Canadian aid package was the loan to Britain negotiated early in 1946. If they were to trade with Canada, British negotiators said, if they were not to be forced to fall back on restrictive practices and on commerce only within a sealed-off Sterling Area, they had to borrow dollars.[3] Certainly Britain had suffered economically during the war. Great Britain had lost a quarter of her prewar wealth and had become the world's largest debtor. Capital assets abroad had been sold off to pay for the war, and even the British merchant fleet was 30 per cent smaller than in 1939.[4] The United Kingdom was almost on the ropes.

Contentious negotiations in Washington had finally led to arrangements for a loan from the United States of $3.75 billion in December 1945 – with humiliating conditions.[5] The British demands of Canada were for fewer dollars, but for far more than the usual 17:1 ratio that differentiated the American national income from the Canadian. London needed almost $2 billion all told, part of a complicated arrangement involving the write-off of war debts on both sides as well as a straight dollar loan. The negotiations were argumentative, the British insisting again and again that while they wanted to buy Canadian goods, they could not do so without dollars. The Canadian ministers and officials had fought among themselves over the terms, but Prime Minister Mackenzie King, always a sentimental imperialist and monarchist at heart, Donald Creighton notwithstanding, helped tip the balance in the direction of generosity. As King wrote in his diary, 'It certainly will be difficult for my political opponents through generations to come to say that I have been anti-British with what has been done for Britain under my administrations in the war and post-war years.'[6] King could not have been more wrong – his political opponents and the historians faced no such difficulty.

Nonetheless, the result was the settlement of all war debts and a loan of $1.25 billion for fifty years at 2 per cent interest – a loan moreover made without humiliating conditions, unless 2 per cent interest could be thought to be humiliating.[7] Incredibly, Canada had given Britain one-third the amount offered by the United States. The loan was also about 10 per cent of the 1946 Gross National Product. That was a testimony to the King government's commitment to the maintenance of Anglo-Canadian trade.

But the loan was not charity to Britain, Finance Minister J.L. Ilsley told the House of Commons: 'it is an investment in the future of Canadian trade.'[8] Progressive Conservative leader John Bracken agreed: the loan was 'essential to the preservation of the Canadian economy as we see it today. Ours is an export economy; we are more than any other country dependent upon foreign nations for a market for our products.'[9] The *Financial Post* made the same point, and then added that it was not simply because the loan had to be spent in Canada for Canadian products that Ottawa had offered it: 'We could just as well have spent the dollars here ourselves.' The loan was made, the business paper said in only slightly hyperbolic terms, to 'afford Britain an opportunity of eventually making a greater contribution to world trade ... The loans, in substance, will act as a lever to get trade moving.'[10]

And trade was moving. Very soon, the difficulty was that too much was coming from the United States into Canada. After ten years of depression and six years of war, Canadians wanted the good things in life. The war had put money into the pockets of farmers who had sold everything they could produce for high prices, of workers who had had as much overtime as they could handle, and of servicemen and women whose pockets bulged with their service gratuities and re-establishment grants. The imports of refrigerators, automobiles, record players, and radios soared, and winter holidays in the American south again became a possibility for the wealthy. The government compounded the difficulty in July 1946 when it raised the Canadian dollar to parity with the American, thus increasing the cost of Canadian exports and encouraging the payment of debts in the United

States.[11] The results became almost immediately apparent in the trade statistics and in Canadian holdings of American dollars. Imports from the United States rose to $1.387 billion in 1946, then the highest peacetime total ever, and the next year they were half as much again. The trade deficit with the United States was $500 million in 1946 and $920 million in 1947.[12] The government's holdings of American dollars, about $1.6 billion in 1946, fell precipitously, sinking to $480 million in November 1947.[13] In the circumstances, every effort to encourage American investment in Canada and sales of metals and minerals to the United States seemed – and was – justified.[14]

This was almost the same situation that had occurred in 1917 and 1941. American dollars, the scarcest commodity in a world of scarcities, were again in short supply. And, as in 1917 and 1941, Canada could not use its surplus in trade with Britain – in 1946, $460 million and in 1947, $560 million – to help redress matters with the United States.[15] The pound sterling, declared convertible for non-residents of the United Kingdom in July 1947 to satisfy the terms of the American loan to Britain, was once more forced into inconvertibility in August when the British government, frightened by a rush of other countries to convert soft sterling into hard dollars, again slapped on controls. Then, the British and the Europeans were using the loan from Canada to pay for the goods they bought in Canada; Canada, in other words, was financing virtually all it sold to Britain and Europe. As A.F.W. Plumptre noted at the time, 'the breakdown of our hopes for selling to England ... for cash was part of a wider breakdown.'[16] Paradoxically, yet predictably, because the Canadian government had wanted to help Britain and Europe and to keep up trade and employment, Canada was in danger of sliding into financial disaster in its relations with the United States.

What was to be done? One possible option was autarky, but no one took this seriously. Another was to join the Sterling Area, the one sure way of expanding trade with Britain and the remnants of empire. But realism had to prevail – in the circumstances of 1947, any alignment with Britain had all the overtones of handcuffing Canada to a corpse. Britain was stopping its aid to Greece and Turkey, abandoning foreign fields to the United States, and the country was on the verge of economic collapse, the Chancellor of the Exchequer 'reaching his wit's end.'[17] In the circumstances, there seemed to be only one possible course for Ottawa: to recognize that Canada was part of the American sphere and to seek a customs union with the United States. Norman Robertson, the wise Canadian high commissioner in Britain, put it best when he asked 'whether we should not ... be thinking of a real reciprocity arrangement with the United States, which would strengthen our dollar position in the short turn, and in the long run, ensure us against too great a dependence, relative to the United States, on the European market. It might be possible to work out a scheme for a graduated approach to reciprocal free trade in a good many commodities on a continental basis, with the steps selected and their depth determined largely by the requirements of our dollar position.'[18] There it was in a nutshell. Canada's dollar shortage, brought on in substantial part by the effort to assist Britain, forced Canada to consider the prospect of reciprocity with the United States. The British government, it is necessary to note, always tended to take Canada's assistance for granted and failed to realize the difficulties Ottawa now found itself in as a result of its aid. That likely explains London's preference for canned salmon from the Soviet Union, timber from Scandinavia, and bacon from Poland. Those countries cheerfully took sterling for their goods, which helped Britain save hard currency dollars for the products it absolutely had to have from North America.[19]

In the meantime, the dollar shortage from which Britain and Canada suffered was a world-wide problem. Britain and Western Europe were in danger of economic collapse, reconstruction was proceeding at a glacial pace, and the Communists in France, Italy, and elsewhere seemed poised to come to power. Western civilization, or so many in Ottawa and Washington believed, seemed as much in danger as it ever had during the war. America's answer was the Marshall Plan, a proposal to give Britain and Europe the dollars they needed to buy American goods. That would rebuild the Continent, check communism, and sell the products of America's factories and farms. But Secretary of State George C. Marshall's plan was only an idea until Congress accepted it.[20]

Even so, there was an opportunity here for Canada. If the Truman administration could be persuaded to use Marshall Plan dollars to pay for Canadian goods, then Canada's dollar shortage could be resolved. There was in this idea a striking parallel to the situation in 1941 when Britain's Lend-Lease account had been charged for the components Canada had to import from the United States so it could manufacture munitions for Britain.

But it was a long way and a longer time from idea to implementation. First, the United States' attention had to be gained. In mid-September 1947, State Department officials concluded that the Canadians 'have been drifting from bad to worse while wishfully thinking that when the time came we would step in and rescue them by means of a loan or procurement devices ... or the Marshall Plan. We cannot, of course, let them go under, but it was time that we explained to them the difficulties on our side.'[21] Not until the end of October, by which time Canadian reserves had dwindled to under a half billion u.s. dollars while the trade deficit widened, did the u.s. administration pay attention. A Canadian delegation to Washington, led by the deputy minister of finance, Clifford Clark, presented two plans for consideration: Plan A hinged around brutal import restrictions and the banning of virtually every identifiable consumer item imported from the United States; Plan B also involved quotas but foresaw Canadian participation in the Marshall Plan and the placing of some procurement for the European recovery program in Canada.[22] The Americans, anxious to avoid the shattering effects on Canadian-American trade certain to be produced by Plan A, promised to make 'a strong stand to obtain the flexibility which they wish in order to make "off-shore procurement" possible.' As a result of this quasi-promise and of discussions that followed in the next days, Finance Minister Douglas Abbott announced the more moderate restrictions of Plan B on 17 November.[23] Abbott pointed to the prospect of Marshall Plan purchases being made in Canada, and he added that 'A program of this kind would resemble in many respects the Hyde Park Agreement that proved so effective and constructive during the war.'[24] Indeed, an arrangement similar to Hyde Park was as necessary in 1947 as it had been in 1941.

At the same time as these discussions were under way, Canadian and American negotiators had begun to consider the possibility of a free-trade agreement. The negotiations went on well into the New Year, and the result was a draft agreement that called for the creation of a modified customs union between the two countries, the immediate removal of all tariffs, and a five-year period in which quantitative restrictions on specified imports could be imposed.[25]

But free trade was not to be – at least, not in 1948. Although he had supported the beginning of negotiations, and although he had seemed enthusiastic as late as 6 March 1948, Mackenzie King had become concerned about the idea of free trade. Henry Luce's *Life* magazine coincidentally had called for a customs union between Canada and the United States on 15 March, and support from that advocate of 'the American Century' was enough to frighten any sensible Canadian. Coincidentally, on 24 March the prime minister had reached onto his bookshelf and pulled down a copy of Richard Jebb's *Studies in Colonial Nationalism*. The book had fallen open at a chapter entitled 'The Soul of Empire.' Would free trade destroy the unity of the empire? King asked himself. Would it weaken the regard in which he was held by his people? Would it let the Conservative party paint him as the man who had sold out Canada to the United States as the culmination of his long political career? 'I would no more think of at my time of life and at this stage of my career attempting any movement of the kind,' King wrote in his diary, 'than I would of flying to the South pole.'[26]

To the chagrin of the few of King's officials who knew of the secret negotiations with the Americans, free trade was dead. The only concession they could get from the old man, still the dominant figure in the country though he was only a few months away from retirement, was the suggestion that if and when a satisfactory 'North Atlantic Security Pact' were reached, then 'It would be natural for the trade discussions to be related to the pact, since they are concerned with measures for economic defence against aggression. It might also turn out,' Hume Wrong, ambassador to the United States, said, 'to be desirable later to add the United Kingdom to such discussions.'[27] The officials' disappointment at the scuttling of free trade almost certainly explains the zeal with which the Department of External Affairs fought to get Article 2, a clause encouraging economic collaboration, into the North Atlantic Treaty.[28]

If free trade were dead, the Marshall Plan lived. The great Economic Cooperation Act, the postwar counterpart to Lend-Lease, passed the Congress on 3 April 1948, speeded in its passage by the Communist coup in Czechoslovakia and by inspired telegrams to Washington from American officials in Germany that foresaw war with the Soviet Union just around the corner. In a first-year appropriation of $5.3 billion, the American Congress allowed 'off-shore procurement' under the act, and the Canadian government seized the opportunity provided. Every conceivable good that could be shipped to Britain and Europe, including wheat Britain had already contracted to buy, seemed to come under the Marshall Plan. 'It will mean no more food for us,' British embassy officials in Washington said, 'and no more money for Canada, but it does mean that shipments will continue at a steady rate with payment guaranteed.'[29]

That was an understatement. The more Marshall Plan aid Britain received, the less strain there would be on the Anglo-Canadian financial relationship. Almost exactly as in 1917 and 1941, the United States gave Britain the dollars it needed to pay for purchases in Canada. The importance of this solution was enormous, exactly as in 1917 and 1941. Now Britain could keep up its contracts with Canada rather than trying to break them in order to get 'free' American aid.[30] Moreover, the Marshall Plan dollars – and Canada received over a billion u.s. dollars over the next two years – meant the resolution of the dollar shortage of November 1947. Canada's success in getting the Truman administration to push for off-shore purchases was a major triumph for Canadian diplomacy – and prairie farmers.

As always, there was a down side to this triumph. Because of Marshall Plan financing of Canadian exports, and because of the high proportion of Canadian exports destined for the United States, an unhealthy part of Canadian eggs were in one, American, basket. An official at the Canadian embassy in Washington who looked at the numbers at the end of 1948 concluded that $2089 million of Canada's total exports of $3045 million went to the United States or were paid for with u.s. Marshall Plan funds. What would happen, he asked, if the Americans changed their policy?[31] No one had an answer, but there should be no doubt about the reasons for the Canadian plight. Canada had been forced to the south by the weakness of the United Kingdom – and the slow pace of Western Europe's reconstruction.

The British soon plunged into yet another financial crisis, and again they moved to reduce imports from Canada as a way of saving dollars. A worried Graham Towers, the governor of the Bank of Canada, put the situation very clearly to London's high commissioner in Ottawa in April 1949. If the British continued to reduce imports from Canada, he said, 'pressures might be set up which might shift the whole outlook of the country towards the United States as the only remaining economic life-line.'[32] Increasingly, Canadian government officials and exporters were obliged to seek trade with the one country able to pay for the goods it imported, the United States; increasingly, the United States was almost Canada's sole paying customer.

That troubled Secretary of State for External Affairs Lester Pearson, for one, although in 1948 he had been an enthusiastic supporter of free trade with the United States. In early 1950 Pearson, a minister for little more than a year and somewhat uncomfortable in criticizing one of the government's giants, told C.D. Howe, the minister of trade and commerce, that 'in the turbulent post-war stream, the current seems to be carrying our boat rather far from its accustomed course, rather too close, perhaps to rocks on one side of the channel.' There was a risk involved in such dependency, 'a rock below the surface,' Pearson argued, and Canada ran the risk of being subjected to American political pressure.

The 'Minister of Everything' was then at the pinnacle of his enormous power, the virtual co-prime minister to Louis St Laurent. Howe was not amused by criticism from External Affairs or from Pearson who was, he thought, 'a little too frightened of the American bogey and, therefore, just a little too anxious to do everything to help the British.'[33] His reply to his junior colleague was brutal in its bluntness. Of course, Canada should try to expand exports to soft currency countries, Howe said, but 'Our export policy should be to sell as much as possible wherever possible. The United States has become the healthiest and most receptive market in the world at a time when intense difficulties are being encountered elsewhere.' Trade with Europe, despite Canada's best efforts, could not equal trade with the Americans. As Howe argued, in words with their own (unconvincing) echo in our own times, 'It is not at all obvious that Canada's sovereignty would be impaired, even by a large increase in the percentage of our exports going to the United States. The surest way to lose our sovereignty,' he concluded, 'would be to get into financial insolvency ... Selling our goods to the Americans is a much better alternative.'[34]

Perhaps Howe was correct – the Gross National Product figures which demonstrated that the United States GNP of $381 billion was more than 500 per cent greater than that of the United Kingdom in 1950 certainly suggested that he was – though the Canadian government made repeated efforts to expand trade with Britain and Europe after 1950.[35] Those efforts, no matter the force with which Canadian negotiators urged the British to make sterling convertible again and to increase imports from Canada, invariably foundered. The United Kingdom, its hard currency reserves in a parlous condition, maintained that it simply could not afford the luxury of imports from a dollar country such as Canada, though, of course, they were willing to export everything possible to this country to earn as many dollars as possible. The problem with expanding sales in Canada was that British export goods too often were badly designed for North America – Vanguard, Austin, and Hillman automobiles that ran poorly in summer and not at all in winter, or apartment-size refrigerators that, unless chained to a steel pipe, moved around the floor every time they were switched on. In any case, as British negotiators baldly told the Canadians, their intention was to decrease imports from Canada even further. They were successful too. British exports to Canada by 1956 were at roughly the same level in constant dollars as in 1913, despite a 450 per cent increase in Canadian imports over the period. Canadian exports to Britain in 1956 were 17 per cent of Canada's total exports; in 1937 they had been 40 per cent. It seemed to be government policy, and also easier for British firms, to import goods from the Sterling Area that Britain, its empire fading away with astonishing rapidity, still dominated economically.[36]

The result on Canada was obvious. Canadian exporters were

forced increasingly, inevitably, to the reliable and rich American market. And Canadian products flooded south while American imports came northwards. Investment funds also came from New York, and American companies established new subsidiaries in Canada. As Bruce Muirhead noted in his able study of Canadian postwar trade policy, 'with Western Europe and Great Britain effectively excluded as possible destinations for billions of dollars worth of Canadian exports, only the United States remained as a market willing and able to absorb a significant amount of Canadian production ... Ottawa took the only course open to it at that time, although not without some qualms and reservations. Henceforth, the United States would become the single most important sun in the Canadian economic constellation, dwarfing in importance all other past or future trading partners.'[37] Ottawa had not become continentalist in its economic policy by choice, Muirhead concluded, but by necessity. 'Ottawa preferred and actively pursued economic multilateralism,' but the British and European response was 'very disappointing, largely because of British post-war economic problems which persisted well into the reconstruction period' and beyond. Ottawa had been 'forced to accept the realities of international trade as it evolved after 1945,' he said, 'which meant that Canada would increasingly move into the American orbit in order to enhance its economic well-being.'[38]

That well-being was most impressive, too, though the Canadian economy had started to falter by the time John Diefenbaker unexpectedly came to power after the election of June 1957. Long disturbed by the increasing American presence in Canada and angered by what he saw as the St Laurent government's abandonment of Britain during the Suez Crisis of the previous fall, the anglophilic Diefenbaker went to London immediately after he assumed office to visit the Queen and attend a Commonwealth Prime Ministers' Conference. When he returned to Canada on 7 July, the cheers of the British still ringing in his ears, he emotionally proclaimed his government's 'planned intention' to divert 15 per cent of Canadian imports from the United States to Britain. Planned intention or not, the prime minister had not consulted the officials in Trade and Commerce or External Affairs before that announcement, and the bureaucrats quickly sent evidence forward that the prime minister's proposal was simply impossible. The British had no capacity to enter half the Canadian import market either because their factories did not produce the goods in question or because their products were inferior to American ones in design, styling, and quality. The General Agreement on Tariffs and Trade also put barriers in the way of any such massive shift. The diversion, in other words, was a policy pronouncement made without any understanding of the facts, and the government backed away from the Chief's unplanned intention very quickly.[39]

Diefenbaker continued to look to Britain, however, though his attitudes began to alter when London decided in 1960 to open negotiations in an effort to join the European Economic Community. A long series of meetings with the British in bilateral and Commonwealth forums ensued, the Canadian rhetoric getting hotter as London drew closer to an acceptable bargain with the EEC.[40] Ottawa's position was curious. Official estimates were that 77 per cent of Canadian industrial exports and about half of all exports to Britain would be unaffected by British entry and, as we have seen, those exports were decreasing in percentage terms with great rapidity.[41] Only Canada's wheat sales to Britain appeared seriously threatened, and there were promising prospects of huge sales to China that held out the hope of averting any prairie dislocation. At a Commonwealth Economic Consultative Council meeting at Accra, Ghana, in September 1961, Finance Minister Donald Fleming and Trade and Commerce Minister George Hees told the delegates that Canada viewed the British negotiations with 'disappointment and grave apprehension' and feared for the Commonwealth's survival. The choice for Britain, the Canadian message went, was either Europe or the Commonwealth.[42]

Diefenbaker ordered his ministers home and roasted them royally for their extreme language, but the Chief soon expressed his own views as vehemently. The prime minister told Britain's Harold Macmillan that Commonwealth preferences were vital to Canada 'as a means of staving off United States domination' and, he added, the Commonwealth was a vital part of the Canadian identity.[43] At a subsequent Commonwealth Prime Ministers' Conference in September 1962, Diefenbaker again denounced the British effort to move into Europe. He argued that the prosperity of every member of the Commonwealth depended on that of Britain, something that was certainly no longer true for Canada. Macmillan had claimed that only the larger market of Europe could let Britain grow but, Diefenbaker said, if that were correct, then it followed that Canada should seek a similar relationship with the United States. Canada, however, had refused to seek economic union with the Americans because that meant a weakening of the ties with Britain and the Commonwealth.[44] Again that was scarcely true. Nonetheless, the Chief had hoisted the by-now tattered flag of empire economic unity, and he drew the cheers of his fellow Commonwealth prime ministers. The *Sunday Observer* reported that 'One of the Ghanaians, as he told the Queen a few nights later, "was so moved that I thought I was going to cry."'[45]

John Diefenbaker, perhaps, might not have turned to the United States once Britain rejected his importunate demands. His relations with the Kennedy administration were not so good as to permit any effort to forge closer economic links with the United States. Even so, at the Commonwealth conference Diefenbaker had slid over some unpleasant facts. When, during and immediately after the election of 1962, there had been a run on the dollar, his government had sent its officials to Washington for loans to bolster Canada's reserves. Despite its dislike of the Diefenbaker government, President Kennedy's administration had arranged the requested funds. In hard economic times, Diefenbaker, just as his predecessors had done, turned to the south for help.[46]

In the end, of course, President Charles de Gaulle blocked British entry into the EEC in January 1963, just days before the Canadian prime minister lost a confidence vote in the Commons on his government's defence policy. Diefenbaker had 'won' the Common Market fight with Britain because the game had been called off, but what had he preserved? Trade with Britain was already small and growing ever smaller in percentage terms. Essentially, it now seems clear, Diefenbaker had been fighting for the idea of Great Britain as it existed in his mind, for the idea of a British Commonwealth and empire that could protect Canada from Americanization. Whether that was any longer a worthy goal or not is immaterial; certainly it was one that no longer had the remotest prospect of realization, as the British, desperately trying to join the Continent, clearly understood. In the context of these essays, however, what is significant is that Britain turned its back on Canada, no matter how much Diefenbaker pleaded with London to reverse the tides of history and save Canada from the United States. For John Diefenbaker, exactly as for Borden, King, and St Laurent before him, Britain's fixed concentration on its own future had left Canada no alternative.[47]

Canada made one further, final, and futile effort to summon up Britain and Europe as a counterweight to the United States. In keeping with its 'Third Option,' the Trudeau government negotiated a contractual link with the European Community in the mid-1970s. The link quite deliberately aimed to increase trade with the EC nations to reduce the nation's increasing reliance on the American market. Though the link was brilliantly negotiated and widely hailed, except in London where the British were noticeably cool to the Canadian plan, unfortunately little resulted from it. Trade with Britain and Europe remained relatively inconsequential in percentage terms thanks to the Common Agricultural Policy, design problems with Canadian goods, and a characteristically lackadaisical effort by Canadian industries to sell their products to the Europeans. Meanwhile, trade with the United States continued to increase in volume. The Europeans might have been to blame for this. Or perhaps Canadian exporters, so accustomed to the relative ease of dealing with the United States, found the difficulties of coping with a multilingual Europe too bothersome to pursue actively. No matter whose fault, the link failed to materialize.[48]

In the area of defence, the close Anglo-Canadian relationship had long since disappeared, to be replaced by what the political scientists call transnational links between the Canadian and American armed forces. After 1945, the British had urged that Ottawa show due caution in joint defence efforts with the United States[49] – a useful warning, but one that lost its force when London tried to persuade the Commonwealth countries to plan for defence together. This was a transparent dodge to have Ottawa, Pretoria, Canberra, and Wellington pay for part of Britain's defence costs or assume some of its shrinking imperial responsibilities. Those attempts went nowhere, Mackenzie King, in particular, scouting the idea as he always had.[50] Nonetheless, Canadian and British troops served together in Korea and cooperated in NATO, though much less so after the Trudeau government's defence cuts of 1969, and a few officers continued to attend staff courses in the United Kingdom. Britain's decline as a world military power had become obvious to everyone after the abortive Suez invasion of 1956.[51] Moreover, the equipment used by the Canadian Armed Forces increasingly was American, as were its tactics and doctrine. Whose fault was this? According to Donald Macdonald, minister of national defence at the beginning of the 1970s, it was Britain's. Macdonald told the *Ottawa Citizen* that the two countries were moving apart 'because this is the way the United Kingdom wants it'; in particular, Prime Minister Edward Heath was actively cutting ties across the Atlantic. 'There used to be the old club rules related to the Commonwealth but Heath doesn't feel they obtain anymore,' Macdonald said. As a result, 'it was natural Canada would get into the stream of American military equipment.' But, the minister added, 'we have to be very wary the Pentagon doesn't pull a snow job on us.'[52] Wary or not, there would be snow jobs aplenty.

Thus, the end of this melodrama. The simple truth is that Canada has had little success in its efforts to find markets or links abroad to act as a counterweight to those with the United States. The Mulroney government has resolved this difficulty in its own collective mind by opting for a free-trade arrangement with the United States. This is not the place to argue the merits or demerits of the particular deal that Simon Reisman and Derek Burney negotiated. But these essays should demonstrate how we reached the point where a Canadian government might think it necessary to seek such an arrangement.

In this century, Canadian governments, Conservative and Liberal, repeatedly tried to maintain and strengthen their trade, economic, and defence relationship with Britain. They assisted the mother country with men, loans, and gifts in two world wars and at the onset of the Cold War, and the British were duly grateful; but not so grateful that they would hesitate to press Canada to the south when it served their interests; nor so grateful that they could help Canada resist the inexorable tug of continentalism. Canada's herculean attempts to aid Britain forced this country's sweet surrender to the United States, with London cheering our governments on. The Americans opened their arms to us, and their embrace was a gentle one. It was a close embrace all the same, one that proved indissoluble. Donald Creighton's argument notwithstanding, it was not Mackenzie King and the Liberal party that sold us out and forced Canada into the arms of the United States, but Great Britain's economic and military decline.

Did and do the Americans want us in their arms? Dean Acheson, the son of Canadian parents, was a friendly yet unforgiving critic of Canada – the 'stern daughter of the Voice of God,' in his words. He once wrote that Canadians were 'a tribal society, naive, terribly serious about the wrong things and not at all aware of their real problems ... Their best move would be to ask us to take them over; and our best move would be to say, no.'[53] I hope Acheson was right in predicting the best American move, for it looks as if we are now asking to be taken over. It must also be said that it is not the Liberal party that is doing the asking.

I began these essays in a deliberately melodramatic fashion. 'You must pay the rent.' 'I can't pay the rent.' The old landlord drove our heroine out into the cold, obliging her to try to fight off the advances of he who had always coveted her. In classic Victorian melodrama, the heroine was always rescued at the end of the last act by the hero, pure, chaste, and noble. But no one can play hero for Canada, I regret to say, as we come to the end of the last act, mine if not yet Canada's. Henceforth, we will all surely pay the rent.

Notes

1 PAVED WITH GOOD INTENTIONS

I am greatly indebted to Dr Norman Hillmer and Professors Ian Drummond, John Saywell, and Bruce Muirhead for their comments on all or parts of these essays. They have saved me from many slips of fact and interpretation.

1 This argument has its mirror in Correlli Barnett, *The Collapse of British Power* (London 1972), 181: 'Domestic and political pressures and personal prejudices alike ... impelled Mackenzie King to set out to break up the "white" empire as an effective alliance; not directly and deliberately, but as the by-product of achieving complete freedom of action for Canada.'

2 W.L. Morton, *The Kingdom of Canada* (Toronto 1963)

3 Review of *William Lyon Mackenzie King*, vol. II, in *Canadian Historical Review* 45 (Dec. 1964), 320–1

4 George Grant, *Lament for a Nation: The Defeat of Canadian Nationalism* (Toronto 1965), 5, 32–3. Grant died on 27 September 1988, and his obituary in the *Globe and Mail* (28 Sept.) said that he had 'despised' the Liberals and quoted him to this effect: 'It was under a Liberal regime that Canada became a branch-plant society. It was under Liberal leadership that our independence in defence and foreign affairs was finally broken.'

5 D.G. Creighton, 'Macdonald and the Anglo-Canadian Alliance,' in

his *Towards the Discovery of Canada* (Toronto 1972), 22–3

6 Donald Creighton, *Canada's First Century* (Toronto 1970), 352–3. In his 'Decline and Fall of the Empire of the St. Lawrence,' Canadian Historical Association, *Papers 1969*, 21, Creighton blames Winston Churchill and Mackenzie King for failing to revive the Anglo-Canadian alliance.

7 See, as examples, Kari Levitt, *Silent Surrender* (Toronto 1970); D. Godfrey and M.H. Watkins, eds., *Gordon to Watkins to You* (Toronto 1970); and James Laxer, *Decline of the Superpowers* (Toronto 1987), 120–1.

8 *Ottawa Citizen*, 18 Dec. 1974, quoted in Norman Hillmer, 'From Bosom to Bony Lap,' *Acadiensis* 11 (autumn 1981), 172

9 Borden was not blind to the dangers of imperialism, however. On a visit to England in 1912 he went to a country weekend organized by the Round Table, perfervid imperialists all, where he was 'propositioned' on the benefits to Canada and to himself of a closer and more tangible imperial connection. 'Impracticable,' Sir Robert growled to his diary, 'and any advantage too remote and indirect.' Cited in Robert Bothwell and John English, 'The View From Inside Out: Canadian Diplomats and Their Public,' *International Journal* 39 (winter 1983–4), 49. For u.s. views on reciprocity in 1911 see Robert Hannigan, 'Reciprocity 1911: Continentalism and American Weltpolitik,' *Diplomatic History* 4 (winter 1980), 1ff. Gordon Stewart, '"A Special Contiguous Country Economic Regime": An Overview of America's Canada Policy,' *Diplomatic History* 6 (fall 1982), 345–6, notes that as early as 1906, u.s. officials foresaw that Canadian attempts to remain part of an imperial economic system would fail.

10 Sir Thomas White, *The Story of Canada's War Finance* (Montreal 1921), 17. See also O.D. Skelton, 'Canadian War Finance,' *American Economic Review* 7 (Dec. 1917), 820.

11 *Documents on Canadian External Relations* (DCER), vol. 1 (Ottawa 1967), 61

12 Ibid., 80–4. See White, *Canada's War Finance*, 19ff, and F.A. Knox, 'Canadian War Finance and the Balance of Payments, 1914–18,' *Canadian Journal of Economics and Political Science* 6 (1940), table iv, which shows provincial borrowing in the United States at $4.3 million, railway securities sales at $14.2 million, and other corporate

securities sales at $12.4 million in the United States in 1914.

13 White, *Canada's War Finance*, 19

14 By 1917, Canada's net capital imports from the United Kingdom were in deficit while a surplus of $138.2 million had come from u.s. sources. Placing of federal government securities in the United States amounted to $100.5 million in 1916, $140.4 million in 1917, and $25 million in 1918. Knox, 'Canadian War Finance,' tables iv, vii

15 See White's comments on the New York market in *Canada's War Finance*, 20.

16 Fred W. Field, 'Retrospect and Prospect,' *Monetary Times* 60 (4 Jan. 1918), 8

17 DCER, vol. 1, 84

18 J.J. Deutsch, 'War Finance and the Canadian Economy, 1914–20,' *Canadian Journal of Economics and Political Science* 6 (1940), 529. See also Michael Bliss, *A Canadian Millionaire* (Toronto 1978), chap. 12ff.

19 See, for example, DCER, vol. 1, 91, 130; Queen's University Archives, J.W. Flavelle Papers, vol. 24, as quoted in Flavelle to R.H. Brand, 4 Aug. 1916

20 National Archives of Canada (NA), Sir Thomas White Papers, vol. 8, White to Flavelle, 7 Nov. 1916

21 Paul Kennedy, *The Rise and Fall of the Great Powers* (Toronto 1987), 268

22 David Lloyd George, *War Memoirs* (London 1933), vol. III, 1699

23 DCER, vol. 1, 170

24 Ibid., 171

25 Ibid., 171ff. See also NA, Department of Finance Records, vol. 761, file 304-1A-1, White memo, 3 Sept. 1917.

26 Ibid., documents on file 304-1A-1; DCER, vol. 1, 176

27 United States National Archives (USNA), Treasury Department Records, RG 39, 'Canada' Country file, box 24, White to W.G. McAdoo, 21 June 1917; DCER, vol. 1, 172. Whether Canada truly was in desperate need of US exchange is less certain. The assets of the chartered banks, including gold, were increasing and the dominion's gold reserves were not decreasing. The deficit with the United States was substantially a product of inflation, and while this caused Canada difficulties, they were scarcely insuperable. I am indebted to Professor Ian Drummond for this information.

28 Treasury Department Records, box 24, White to McAdoo, 21 June 1917
29 Ibid.
30 White Papers, vol. 18, White to George Foster, 28 April 1917
31 David Carnegie, *The History of Munitions Supply in Canada* (London 1925), 219ff; Bliss, *Canadian Millionaire*, 365ff; Flavelle Papers, documents on vols. 24, 26, 34, 54; White Papers, vol. 3, Flavelle to Borden, 7 Nov. 1917
32 *Financial Post*, 3 Nov. 1917
33 See R.D. Cuff and J.L. Granatstein, *Canadian-American Relations in Wartime* (Toronto 1975), chap. 3.
34 *Financial Post*, 15 Dec. 1917
35 Henry Borden, ed., *Robert Laird Borden: His Memoirs* (Toronto 1938), vol. ii, 772–3
36 F.H. Leacy, ed., *Historical Statistics of Canada* (Ottawa 1983), G188–202
37 M.C. Urquhart and K.A.H. Buckley, eds., *Historical Statistics of Canada* (Toronto 1965), F348–56

2 STARING INTO THE ABYSS

1 See Philip Wigley, *Canada and the Transition to Commonwealth: British-Canadian Relations 1917–1926* (Cambridge 1977), 129ff. D.C. Watt erroneously saw 'geographical or racialist factors' responsible for 'the pro-American orientation' of Canadian foreign policy, and he argued that British actions here were taken 'for the sake of keeping Canada in the Empire.' *Succeeding John Bull: America in Britain's Place 1900–1975* (Cambridge 1984), 50, 52
2 King expressed strong support for the effort to widen imperial preferences at the Imperial Economic Conference of 1923. See R.M. Dawson, *William Lyon Mackenzie King*, vol. i: *A Political Biography 1874–1923* (Toronto 1958), 469ff. The 1930 Liberal budget lowered the duties on 270 British goods exported to Canada and threatened countervailing duties against the United States. See H.B. Neatby, *William Lyon Mackenzie King*, vol. ii: *The Lonely Heights* (Toronto 1963), 323–4. On reaction to u.s. investment in this period and after see Peter Kresl, 'Before the Deluge: Canadians on Foreign Ownership, 1920–1955,' *American Review of Canadian Studies* 6 (spring 1976), 86ff.

3 Quoted in Norman Hillmer, 'Personalities and Problems in Anglo-Canadian Economic Relations between the Two World Wars,' *Bulletin of Canadian Studies* 3 (June 1979), 5, 8

4 Peter Kasurak, 'American Foreign Policy Officials and Canada, 1927–1941: A Look Through Bureaucratic Glasses,' *International Journal* 32 (summer 1977), 548

5 The best study of the Ottawa Conference, including its origins and aftermath, is in Ian Drummond, *Imperial Economic Policy 1917–1939* (London 1974), chap. 5ff.

6 C.P. Stacey, *Mackenzie King and the North Atlantic Triangle* (Toronto 1976), chap. 2

7 Correlli Barnett, *The Collapse of British Power* (London 1972), 195. Barnett's index reference under Mackenzie King refers to this episode as 'destroys imperial alliance.' Stacey's judgment is more sensible and accurate: King 'challenged this idea of a common foreign policy and, essentially, destroyed it.' Stacey, *Mackenzie King*, 33

8 'Gentlemen vs Players,' *New York Review of Books* (29 Sept, 1988), 63

9 Donald Creighton, 'The Decline and Fall of the Empire of the St. Lawrence,' *Historical Papers 1969*, 21

10 Within a year of giving up the Conservative party leadership, Bennett left Canada to live in England. 'It's grand to be going home,' the New Brunswick-born Bennett said as he left for the mother country. That may have been the most revealing comment ever made about Canadian Conservatism prior to the Second World War. Bennett soon violated Canadian law by accepting a peerage.

11 F.D. Roosevelt Library, Roosevelt Papers, PSF, box 33, Armour to Phillips, 22 Oct. 1935

12 On the decline in British trade see Paul Kennedy, *The Rise and Fall of the Great Powers* (Toronto 1987), 316. On the Canadian-American trade agreements see J.L. Granatstein, *A Man of Influence* (Ottawa 1981), chap. 3, and R.N. Kottman, *Reciprocity and the North Atlantic Triangle, 1932–1938* (Ithaca 1968).

13 This is the subject of Gregory Johnson's York University doctoral dissertation in progress on the relations of Canada, the United States, and the United Kingdom in the Pacific from 1935 to 1950.

14 R.F. Swanson, *Canadian-American Summit Diplomacy, 1923–1973* (Toronto 1975), 52ff. According to D.C. Watt, Mackenzie King was

'yet another channel by which disguised isolationist ideas could be fed to the president.' *Succeeding John Bull*, 78

15 M.C. Urquhart and K.A.H. Buckley, eds., *Historical Statistics of Canada* (Toronto 1965), F345–56; F.H. Leacy, ed., *Historical Statistics of Canada* (Ottawa 1983), G188–202. I have used 1939 data, though Canada's trade with the United States was higher then than throughout the rest of the decade since that was the first year that showed the impact of the 1938 trade agreement. In other words, had the Second World War not distorted trade patterns, the 1939 trends would likely have continued.

16 *Globe Magazine*, 15 Aug. 1970, quoted in Norman Hillmer, ' "The Outstanding Imperialist": Mackenzie King and the British,' Part I of *Britain and Canada in the Age of Mackenzie King*, Canada House Lecture Series No 4 [1979], 3–4

17 Stacey, *Mackenzie King*, 68

18 National Archives of Canada (NA), Robert Borden Papers, Note by Loring Christie, nd, f 148398

19 L.L.L. Golden interview, 3 Oct. 1965

20 NA, John W. Dafoe Papers, Grant Dexter to Dafoe, 18 April 1941

21 Hugh Hood, *The Swing in the Garden* (Toronto 1975), 165

22 The fate of the Royal Navy naturally concerned the United States and involved Mackenzie King in an excruciating role between Churchill and Roosevelt. See David Reynolds, *The Creation of the Anglo-American Alliance 1937–1941* (Chapel Hill, NC 1982), 115ff, for an American historian's view.

23 Barnett nonetheless argues that the presence of a Canadian corps in England did not make up for the dispatch of British troops to the Middle and Far East. 'The nations of the empire were true "daughters" of the Mother Country in that at no time during the war did their contributions defray the cost of their own strategic keep.' Barnett, *Collapse*, 586. In his later book, *The Audit of War* (London 1986), 3, he adds that the empire produced only 10 per cent of the munitions of war supplied to British and imperial forces. So much for Canada's unstinted contribution to the war.

24 D.G. Creighton, 'The Ogdensburg Agreement and F.H. Underhill,' in C. Berger and R. Cook, eds., *The West and the Nation* (Toronto 1976), 303

25 NA, Department of External Affairs Records (EAR), vol. 781, file 394, 'An Outline Synopsis,' 17 June 1940
26 NA, W.L.M. King Papers, Black Binders, vol. 19, Christie to King, 15 Aug. 1940. Reynolds, *Creation*, 118, describes FDR's request for the Ogdensburg meeting as being necessary to formulate 'contingency plans in case Britain lost control of the North Atlantic.' See also Reynolds, *Creation*, 132, 183.
27 J.W. Pickersgill, ed., *The Mackenzie King Record*, vol. 1: *1939–44* (Toronto 1960), 130–1
28 Ibid., 134
29 Thomas Keneally, *The Cut-Rate Kingdom* (London 1984), 125. This novel of Australia's experience with, among other things, the United States in the Second World War has some useful and suggestive parallels for the Canadian case.
30 Ibid., 14
31 J.L. Granatstein, *Canada's War: The Politics of the Mackenzie King Government, 1939–45* (Toronto 1975), 131–2
32 Gerard S. Vano has suggested that there had been a reversal of military obligation within the empire by this period. No longer was Canada under the British military shield, but 'Britain was, to a degree, falling under a Canadian shield.' *Canada: The Strategic and Military Pawn* (New York 1988), 87. Reynolds, *Creation*, 136, notes that Australia and New Zealand, as well as Canada, were forced closer to the United States by the events of the summer of 1940.
33 NA, R.B. Hanson Papers, file S-175-M-1, Meighen to Hanson, 19 Aug. 1940
34 Professor Underhill, who spoke the truth about the changed Canadian relationships produced by the war, almost lost his job at the University of Toronto as a result. See Creighton, 'Ogdensburg Agreement,' 300ff, and Douglas Francis, *F.H. Underhill: Intellectual Provocateur* (Toronto 1986), chap. 10.
35 NA, Privy Council Office Records, Cabinet War Committee Records, Documents, Churchill to King, 22 Aug. 1940
36 Even the usually shrewd observer of Canadian-American relations, Gordon Stewart, has missed this key point. He noted that in the 1940s, Canada 'participated willingly in military and defense integration … it is inaccurate to regard American policy as being imposed

on an unwilling and unknowing country. If the United States is judged guilty of imperialism, then Canada must accept a ruling of contributory negligence.' '"A Special Contiguous Country Economic Regime": An Overview of America's Canada Policy,' *Diplomatic History* 6 (fall 1982), 354–5. True enough, but Britain aided and abetted the process. John Warnock in *Free Trade and the New Right Agenda* (Vancouver 1988), 255, notes similarly that 'The Mackenzie King government chose to conduct the war effort on a continental basis' and thus 'greatly undermined Canadian sovereignty.' Some choice in August 1940!

37 The King government was slow to recognize the dangers posed to Canadian sovereignty by the u.s. presence. But once it was alerted to the problem (by the British high commissioner to Canada!), it moved quickly to appoint a special commissioner in the northwest and, at war's end, Canada paid the United States in full for all facilities built in Canada – quite consciously in an effort to ensure that its rights were fully protected. See Department of External Affairs, Records [DEA], documents on files 52-B(s), 5221-40C, the records of the special commissioner (NA, RG 36–7), and Granatstein, *A Man of Influence*, 120ff.

38 George Grant, *Lament for a Nation* (Toronto 1965), 50

39 Cited in David Dilks, 'Appeasement Revisited,' *University of Leeds Review* 15 (May 1972), 51

40 Based on Hector Mackenzie, 'Sinews of War: Aspects of Canadian Decisions to Finance British Requirements in Canada during the Second World War,' Canadian Historical Association paper 1983, 3

41 King Papers, W.C. Clark to King, 9 April 1941, ff 288021ff

42 H.D. Hall, *North American Supply* (London 1955), 230. Later, more accurate assessments put war spending in 1941–42 at $1.45 billion, aid to the United Kingdom at $1.15 billion, and civil expenditures at $1 billion. With a national income of $5.95 billion, public expenditure amounted to 60.5 per cent. King Papers, 'Canada's War Effort,' 4 April 1941, ff 288088ff

43 The phrase is R.S. Sayers's in *Financial Policy, 1939–45* (London 1956), 322–3. The balance, however, was less than real for the British. They had large peacetime trade deficits with the United States and could pay Canada in u.s. dollars only because they received

them from other parties in a pattern of multilateral settlement that ended with the outbreak of war. I am indebted to Professor Ian Drummond for this information.

44 King Papers, Clark to King, 9 April 1941, ff 288014ff. The actual figures were even worse than these estimates. See Urquhart and Buckley, eds., *Historical Statistics*, F334-47. But whether the situation was as bleak as government officials believed at the time is less certain. Although munitions exports to Britain did stimulate the growth of imports from the United States, still more came from the war effort itself, which stimulated imports directly (in the form of components) and indirectly (by increasing consumer demand and domestic investment in plant and equipment). I am again indebted to Professor Drummond.

45 Granatstein, *Canada's War*, 135–6; Granatstein, *A Man of Influence*, 94ff

46 EAR, vol. 35, 'United States Exchange Discussions,' 20 Nov. 1940

47 Urquhart and Buckley, eds., *Historical Statistics*, F164–92; King Papers, Clark to King, 9 April 1941, ff 288018ff; Queen's University Archives, Grant Dexter Papers, Memorandum, 11 March 1941

48 On the costs to the United Kingdom see Barnett, *Collapse*, 591ff. Churchill was asked if Britain would be able to repay the United States for its aid: 'I shall say, yes by all means let us have an account if we can get it reasonably accurate, but I shall have my account to put in too, and my account is for holding the baby alone for eighteen months, and it was a very rough brutal baby.' Quoted in David Dilks's introduction to Dilks, ed., *Retreat from Power*, vol. II: *After 1939* (London 1981), 14

49 Robert Bothwell and John English, 'Canadian Trade Policy in the Age of American Dominance and British Decline, 1943–1947,' *Canadian Review of American Studies* 8 (spring 1977), 54ff. A.F.W. Plumptre commented that 'Ottawa apparently believed that it is well to keep Canada as independent as possible and to avoid borrowing or begging as long as may be.' *Mobilizing Canada's Resources for War* (Toronto 1941), 80. Cf R.W. James, *Wartime Economic Cooperation* (Toronto 1949), 32

50 Cabinet War Committee Records, Minutes, 18, 26 Feb. 1941

51 Public Record Office (PRO), London, Prime Minister's Office Records,

PREM 4/43B/2, Cranborne to Churchill, 5 March 1941; ibid., Treasury Records, T160/1340, Amery to Kingsley Wood, 10 May 1941

52 Ibid., T160/1054, 'Canadian Financial Assistance to this Country,' nd [14 March 1941]

53 Granatstein, *Canada's War*, 139

54 Cabinet War Committee Records, Minutes, 12, 13 March 1941; Sayers, *Financial Policy*, 338ff

55 Dexter Papers, Memo, 21 April 1941

56 The text of the Hyde Park Agreement is printed as an appendix to R.D. Cuff and J.L. Granatstein, *Canadian-American Relations in Wartime* (Toronto 1975), 165–6.

57 Pickersgill, ed., *Mackenzie King Record*, I, 202

58 C.P. Stacey, *Arms, Men and Governments* (Ottawa 1970), 490; Richard Rohmer, *E.P. Taylor* (Toronto 1978), 106

59 This was seen as a virtual miracle. See *Financial Post*, 26 April 1941.

60 See J.L. Granatstein, 'Settling the Accounts: Anglo-Canadian War Finance, 1943–1945,' *Queen's Quarterly*, 83 (summer 1976), 246.

61 PRO, Dominions Office Records, DO35/1218, Minute by A.W. Snelling, 26 Jan. 1943; Sayers, *Financial Policy*, 350ff

62 S.D. Pierce and A.F.W. Plumptre, 'Canada's Relations with War-Time Agencies in Washington,' *Canadian Journal of Economics and Political Science* 11 (1945), 410–11

63 Urquhart and Buckley, eds., *Historical Statistics*, F345–56; Leacy, ed., *Historical Statistics*, G188–202

3 OVER THE EDGE

1 Donald Creighton, *The Forked Road: Canada 1939–1957* (Toronto 1976), 187. Some contemporary British writers have come to recognize that Britain, bereft of power though it may have been in 1945, still tried to treat Canada as a colonial appendage. See, for example, Hugh Thomas, *Armed Truce* (London 1988), 292–3.

2 James Laxer, *Decline of the Superpowers* (Toronto 1987), 120–1

3 The British by 1944 were calculating how best to reduce purchases in Canada: 'In certain cases the Canadian position should be satisfactorily met by the proposed long-term contracts, tapered off when suitable ... in other cases we are apparently looking to switch pretty

completely from Canadian to European sources of supply as soon as we can.' PRO, Treasury Records, T160/1376, Clutterbuck to Robertson, 24 April 1944. Eventually, this policy led the United Kingdom to consider 'whether it was right to "save foreign exchange" by importing bauxite and manufacturing it into aluminum here at a cost far above that of imported Canadian aluminum.' Sir Richard Clarke, *Anglo-American Economic Collaboration in War and Peace 1942–1949* (Oxford 1982), 60. On the loan negotiations and the discussions preceding it see the fine memoir by Douglas LePan, *Bright Glass of Memory* (Toronto 1979), chap. 2, and Alec Cairncross, *Years of Recovery: British Economic Policy 1945–51* (London 1985). The official British version of postwar financial relations which, unlike most British studies, actually pays some attention to Canada and the Canadian loan is L.S. Pressnell, *External Economic Policy Since the War*, vol. 1 (London 1986).

4 Thomas, *Armed Truce*, 316

5 See R.N. Gardner, *Sterling-Dollar Diplomacy* (New York 1969). 'Humiliating conditions' is Thomas's phrase; *Armed Truce*, 316.

6 J.W. Pickersgill and D.F. Forster, *The Mackenzie King Record*, vol. III: *1945–46* (Toronto 1970), 175

7 Pressnell, *External Economic Policy*, 343ff; Hector Mackenzie, 'The Path to Temptation: The Negotiation of Canada's Reconstruction Loan to Britain in 1946,' Canadian Historical Association, *Papers, 1982,* 196ff

8 House of Commons, *Debates,* 11 April 1946, 772

9 Ibid., 16 April 1946, 929. The CCF and Social Credit leaders supported the loan as well.

10 *Financial Post,* 22 June 1946. See also A.F.W. Plumptre, *Three Decades of Decision* (Toronto 1977), 74ff.

11 On the dollar see Queen's University Archives, W.A. Mackintosh Papers, box 4, 'A Note on the Canadian Dollar,' nd.

12 F.H. Leacy, ed., *Historical Statistics of Canada* (Ottawa 1983), G401–14. There is a breakdown of the components of the balance of payments with the United States in R.D. Cuff and J.L. Granatstein, *American Dollars – Canadian Prosperity* (Toronto 1978), 30–1.

13 See National Archives of Canada (NA), C.D. Howe Papers, vol. 87, file S48-10, 'The Canadian Exchange Problem,' 18 Aug. 1947; R.C.

McIvor and J.H. Panabaker, 'Canadian Post-war Monetary Policy 1946–52,' *Canadian Journal of Economics and Political Science* (CJEPS) 20 (May 1954), 215; J. Douglas Gibson, 'Post-War Economic Developments and Policy in Canada,' CJEPS 20 (Nov. 1954), 446–7.

14 See Cuff and Granatstein, *American Dollars*, chap. 5. It is worth noting that even while Canada scrambled for U.s. dollars, quantities of scarce raw materials were reserved for the British market.

15 Leacy, ed., *Historical Statistics*, G401–14

16 A.F.W. Plumptre, 'Detour into Controls,' *International Journal* 3 (winter 1947–8), 3. The British Treasury looked at Canada's dire dollar situation in July 1947 and concluded that 'Help for Canada is important to us in order to enable the Canadians to continue to let us draw on their Credit, and, indeed, in order to let them lend us more.' Clarke, *Anglo-American Economic Collaboration*, 172

17 David Dilks's phrase in the introduction to his *Retreat from Power*, vol. II: *After 1939* (London 1981), 22.

18 Department of External Affairs [DEA], Records, file 264(s), Robertson to L.B. Pearson, 19 June 1947. See also Denis Smith, *Diplomacy of Fear: Canada and the Cold War 1941–48* (Toronto 1988), 197–8, for Dana Wilgress's views of the situation.

19 Based on Bruce Muirhead, 'Canadian Trade Policy, 1949–57,' book ms, chap. 1, 28

20 A dispatch from Washington analysing the administration's difficulties is DEA, file 264(s), Hume Wrong to secretary of state for external affairs, 26 Sept. 1947.

21 United States National Archives (USNA), Department of State Records, 842.5151/9-1847, A.B. Foster to C.T. Wood et al., 18 Sept. 47

22 Ibid., 842.5151/11-147, 'Memorandum for the Files,' 1 Nov. 1947; DEA, file TS 265(s), Tel., Canadian ambassador to secretary of state for external affairs, 1 Nov. 1947, and 'Summary of U.s.-Canadian Financial Discussions, November 1, 1947'

23 See, on these negotiations, J.L. Granatstein and R.D. Cuff, 'Canada and the Marshall Plan, June–December 1947,' *Historical Papers 1977*, 197ff. The restrictions reduced imports from the United States by $153 million in 1948. Leacy, ed., *Historical Statistics*, G408–14. See also Robert Bothwell and William Kilbourn, *C.D. Howe: A Biography* (Toronto 1979), 234–5.

24 NA, D.C. Abbott Papers, vol. 16, file 48, text
25 See Robert Cuff and J.L. Granatstein, 'The Rise and Fall of Canadian-American Free Trade, 1947–8,' *Canadian Historical Review* 57 (Dec. 1977), 459ff.
26 NA, W.L.M. King Papers, Diary, 24 March 1948. King was wiser than he knew. Willard Thorp, assistant secretary of state for economic affairs and an American participant in the free-trade talks, told his superiors that the agreement offered 'a unique opportunity of promoting the most efficient utilization of the resources of the North American continent and knitting the two countries together – an objective of U.S. foreign policy since the founding of the republic.' Thorp to Lovett, 8 March 1948, *Foreign Relations of the United States 1948* (Washington 1972), IX, 406
27 State Department Records, FW611.422/10-2649, Wrong to J. Hickerson, 1 April 1948
28 See J.L. Granatstein, *A Man of Influence* (Ottawa 1981), 236–7, for the origins of this idea.
29 Montreal *Star*, 6 May 1948. Canada and off-shore purchases go unmentioned in Forrest Pogue's *George C. Marshall: Statesman 1945–59* (New York 1987).
30 See DEA, file 264(s), Memo for Moran, 16 April 1948; ibid., Robertson to Clark, 19 April 1948.
31 EAR, Washington Embassy files, vol. 2158, 'Economic Cooperation' file, Murray to Wrong, 20 Dec. 1948
32 Dominions Office Records, Sir A. Clutterbuck's 'Note of a Private and Confidential Conversation with Governor and Deputy-Governor of Bank of Canada,' 14 April 1949, as quoted in Bruce Muirhead, 'Trials and Tribulations: The Decline of Anglo-Canadian Trade, 1945–50,' unpublished paper, 14
33 Bank of Canada, Bank of Canada Records, file 5D-450, 'Comments by C.D. Howe on Mr. Pearson's Memorandum entitled "A Review of Measures to Promote Canadian Exports to Soft Currency Countries,"' 21 April 1950. I am indebted to Bruce Muirhead for this reference. Howe, moreover, had come over time to see the British as unreliable partners. 'They would, in his view,' Robert Bothwell wrote of dealings in atomic energy matters, 'take any way out of a deal, and leave the Canadians to pick up the tab ... The Americans, as Howe knew,

had more more money, and that made it easier to deal with them.'
Eldorado (Toronto 1984), 195–6

34 Howe Papers, vol. 4, file s4–12, Pearson's 'A Review of Measures to
Promote Canadian Exports ...' 19 April 1950; ibid., 'Comments by
C.D. Howe ...' 21 April 1950; Bothwell and Kilbourn, *Howe*, 236–7

35 Paul Kennedy, *The Rise and Fall of the Great Powers* (New York 1987),
369. UK GNP (in 1964 dollars) in 1950 was $71 billion. British per
capita GNP was just above half that of the United States.

36 Based on Bruce Muirhead, 'Canadian Trade Policy, 1949–57: The
Failure of the Anglo-European Option,' PhD thesis, York University, 1986; Urquhart and Buckley, eds., *Historical Statistics*, F334–47

37 Muirhead, 'Canadian Trade Policy,' 13

38 Ibid., 16

39 See J.L. Granatstein, *Canada 1957–1967: Indecision and Innovation*
(Toronto 1986), 44–5. On the impossibility of the trade diversion see
NA, Gordon Churchill Papers, vol. 14, 'Diversion of Canadian
Imports,' 9 Aug. 1957.

40 See, for example, *Globe and Mail*, 14, 21 June 1961, 17 April 1962, 12
Sept. 1962.

41 NA, George Drew Papers, vol. 390, Memos attached to Green to
Drew, 17 July 1961

42 Peyton Lyon, *Canada in World Affairs 1961–63* (Toronto 1968), 448–9.
For Donald Fleming's account of the Accra conference and the sub-
sequent flap see *So Very Near: The Political Memoirs of the Hon. Donald
M. Fleming*, vol. II: *The Summit Years* (Toronto 1985), 389ff.

43 DEA, file 12447-40, Record of Meeting, 30 April 1962

44 Green Papers, vol. 7, Minutes of Meeting of Commonwealth Prime
Ministers 1962, 11 Sept. 1962

45 *Sunday Observer* [UK], 16 Sept. 1962

46 See Granatstein, *Canada 1957–67*, chap. 4.

47 A few years later, the British complained about what Prime Minister
Pearson called the 'very strong' Canadian 'export performance in
the British market' and their own 'rather poor showing' in the Canadian market. To Pearson it did 'seem inescapable to us that their
weakness in trade with Canada reflects a broader weakness in the
British economy as a whole.' Those complaints, and implied threats
of action to curb Canadian export success, inevitably focused Cana-

dian attention southwards. NA, Department of Trade and Commerce Records, vol. 58, UK General file, Pearson to L. Chevier, 14 April 1966 (draft). I am indebted to Dr Gustav Schmidt for this reference.

48 This paragraph is based on a work in progress by Granatstein and Robert Bothwell on Trudeau's foreign policy, 1968–84.

49 See Smith, *Diplomacy of Fear*, 170.

50 Elisabeth Barker, *The British between the Superpowers 1949–50* (Toronto 1983), 58–60, 137–8

51 On Suez see John English and Norman Hillmer, 'Canada's Alliances,' *Revue internationale d'histoire militaire* 54 (1982), 38–9.

52 *Ottawa Citizen*, 23 Feb. 1971

53 David McClellan and David Acheson, eds., *Among Friends* (New York 1980), 250

Picture Credits

The cartoons appeared in Peter Desbarats and Terry Mosher, *The Hecklers: A History of Canadian Political Cartooning and a Cartoonists' History of Canada* (Toronto: McClelland and Stewart 1979): A Pertinent Question *Diogenes*, 18 June 1869; Coming Home from the Fair *Canadian Illustrated News*, 1876 or 1877; Uncle Sam Toronto *Daily News*; Helping Uncle and Helping Father Newton McConnell, 27 July 1912; Nervous One Ivan Glassco, 22 May 1940

Sir Robert Borden Provincial Archives, Victoria, British Columbia; R.B. Bennett National Film Board; Mackenzie King and Churchill, Quebec 1943 National Archives of Canada, C17288; King, Churchill, Roosevelt, and the Earl of Athlone NFB; Louis St Laurent NA, C21524; C.D. Howe NA, C472; John Diefenbaker Toronto Star Syndicate

Index

THE JOANNE GOODMAN LECTURES

1976
C.P. Stacey, *Mackenzie King and the Atlantic Triangle* (Toronto: Macmillan of Canada/Maclean Hunter Press 1976)

1977
Robin W. Winks, *The Relevance of Canadian History: US and Imperial Perspectives* (Toronto: Macmillan 1979)

1978
Robert Rhodes James, 'Britain in Transition'

1979
Charles Ritchie, 'Diplomacy: The Changing Scene'

1980
Kenneth A. Lockridge, *Settlement and Unsettlement in Early America: The Crisis of Political Legitimacy befor the Revolution* (New York: Cambridge University Press 1981)

1981
Geoffrey Best, *Honour Among Men and Nations: Transformations of an Idea* (Toronto: University of Toronto Press 1982)

1982
Carl Berger, *Science, God, and Nature in Victorian Canada* (Toronto: University of Toronto Press 1983)

1983
Alistair Horne, *The French Army and Politics, 1870–1970* (London: Macmillan 1984)

1984
William Freehling, 'Crisis United States Style: A Comparison of the American Revolutionary and Civil Wars'

1985
Desmond Morton, *Winning the Second Battle: Canadian Veterans and the Return to Civilian Life 1915–1930* (published with Glenn Wright as joint author. Toronto: University of Toronto Press 1987)

1986
J.R. Lander, *The Limitations of the English Monarchy in the Later Middle Ages* (Toronto: University of Toronto Press 1989)

1987
Elizabeth Fox-Genovese, 'The Female Self in the Age of Bourgeois Individualism'

1988
J.L. Granatstein, *How Britain's Weakness Forced Canada into the Arms of the United States* (Toronto: University of Toronto Press 1989)